Good Morning, Holy Spirit

Other books by Benny Hinn

The Anointing

The Biblical Road to Blessing

Welcome, Holy Spirit

He Touched Me

Good Morning, Holy Spirit

Benny Hinn

THOMAS NELSON
Since 1798

NASHVILLE   DALLAS   MEXICO CITY   RIO DE JANEIRO

Published in Nashville, Tennessee, by Thomas Nelson. Thomas Nelson is a registered trademark of Thomas Nelson, Inc.

Scripture quotations are from THE NEW KING JAMES VERSION. Copyright © 1982 Thomas Nelson, Inc. Used by permission. All rights reserved.

The Scripture quotation noted KJV is from the KING JAMES VERSION of the Bible.

Library of Congress Cataloging-in-Publication Data

Control Number: 2003021620

Printed in the United States of America

04 05 06 07 08 PHX 6 5 4 3 2 1

To the person of the Holy Spirit,
who is the very reason for my being

and

To my daughters, Jessica, Natasha, and Eleasha,
and to my son, Joshua,
who, should the Lord tarry,
will carry this message to their generation

Contents

CONTENTS

ONE

"Can I Really Know You?"

It was three days before Christmas 1973. The sun was still rising on that cold, misty Toronto morning.

Suddenly He was there. The Holy Spirit entered my room. He was as real to me that morning as the book you are holding in your hand is to you.

For the next eight hours I had an incredible experience with the Holy Spirit. It changed the course of my life. Tears of wonder and joy coursed down my cheeks as I opened the Scriptures and He gave me the answers to my questions.

It seemed that my room had been lifted into the hemisphere of heaven. And I wanted to stay there forever. I had just turned twenty-one, and this visitation was the best birthday or Christmas present I had ever received.

Just down the hall were my mother and dad. They would never possibly understand what was happening to their Benny. In fact, had they known what I was experiencing, it could have been the breaking point in a family that was already on the verge of shattering. For nearly two years—since the day I gave my life to Jesus—there was virtually no communication between my parents and me. It was horrible. As the son of an immigrant family from Israel, I had humiliated the household by breaking tradition. Nothing else in my life had been this devastating.

In my room, however, it was pure joy. Yes, it was unspeakable. Yes, it was full of glory! If you had told me just forty-eight hours earlier what was about to happen to me, I would have said, "No way." But from that very moment the Holy Spirit became alive in my life. He was no longer a distant "third person" of the Trinity. He was real. He had a personality.

And now I want to share Him with you.

My friend, if you are ready to begin a personal relationship with the Holy Spirit that surpasses anything you ever dreamed possible, read on. If not, let me recommend that you close the covers of this book forever. That's right. Close the book! Because what I am about to share will transform your spiritual life.

Suddenly it will happen to you. It may be while you're reading. Perhaps while you're praying. Or while you're driving to work. The Holy Spirit is going to respond to your invitation. He's going to become your closest friend, your guide, your comforter, your lifelong companion. And when you and He meet, you'll say, "Benny! Let me tell you what the Spirit has been doing in my life!"

God's Power Revealed

A Short Night in Pittsburgh

A friend of mine, Jim Poynter, had asked me to go with him on a charter bus trip to Pittsburgh, Pennsylvania. I had met Jim, a Free Methodist minister, at the church I attended. The group was going to a meeting of a healing evangelist, Kathryn Kuhlman.

To be honest, I knew very little about her ministry. I'd seen her on television, and she totally turned me off. I thought she talked funny and looked a little strange. So I wasn't exactly filled with expectation.

But Jim was my friend, and I didn't want to let him down.

On the bus I said, "Jim, you'll never know what a tough time I had with my father about this trip." You see, after my conversion, my parents had done everything in their power to keep me from attending church. And now a trip to Pittsburgh? It was almost out of the question, but they grudgingly gave their permission.

We left Toronto on Thursday about midmorning. And what should have been a seven-hour trip was slowed by a sudden snowstorm. We didn't arrive at our hotel until one o'clock in the morning.

Then Jim said, "Benny, we have to be up at five."

"Five this morning?" I asked. "What for?"

He told me that if we weren't outside the doors of the building by six o'clock, we'd never get a seat.

Well, I just couldn't believe it. Who'd ever heard of standing in the freezing cold before sunrise to go to church? But he said that was what we were supposed to do.

It was bitter cold. At five I got up and put on every bit of clothing I could find: boots, gloves, the works. I looked like an Eskimo.

We arrived at the First Presbyterian Church, downtown Pittsburgh, while it was still dark. But what shocked me was that hundreds of people were already there. And the doors wouldn't open for two more hours.

Being small has some advantages. I began inching my way closer and closer to the doors—and pulling Jim right behind me. There were even people sleeping on the front steps. A woman told me, "They've been here all night. It's like this every week."

As I stood there, I suddenly began to vibrate—as if someone had gripped my body and begun to shake it.

I thought for a moment that the bitter air had gotten to me. But I was dressed warmly, and I certainly didn't feel too cold. An uncontrollable shaking just came over me.

Nothing like that had ever happened before. And it didn't stop. I was too embarrassed to tell Jim, but I could feel my very bones rattling. I felt it in my knees. In my mouth. *What's happening to me?* I wondered. *Is this the power of God?* I just didn't understand.

Racing through the Church

By this time the doors were about to open, and the crowd pressed forward until I could hardly move. Still the vibrating wouldn't stop.

Jim said, "Benny, when those doors open, run just as fast as you can."

"Why?" I asked.

"If you don't, they'll run right over you." He'd been there before and knew what to expect.

Well, I never thought I'd be in a race going to church, but here I was. And when those doors opened, I took off like an Olympic sprinter. I passed everybody: old women, young men, all of them. In fact, I made it right to the front row and tried to sit down. An usher told me the first row was reserved. I learned later that Miss Kuhlman's staff handpicked the people who sat in the front row. She was so sensitive to the Spirit that she wanted only positive, praying supporters right in front of her.

With my severe stuttering problem, I knew it would be useless to argue with the usher. The second row was already filled, but Jim and I found a spot on row three.

It would be another hour before the service began, so I took off my coat, my gloves, and my boots. As I relaxed, I realized I was shaking more than before. It just wouldn't stop. The vibrations were going through my arms and legs as if I were attached to some kind of a machine. The experience was foreign to me. To be honest, I was scared.

As the organ played, all I could think about was the shaking in my body. It wasn't a "sick" feeling. It wasn't as if I were catching a cold or a virus. In fact, the longer it continued, the more beautiful it became. It was an unusual sensation that didn't really seem physical at all.

At that moment, almost out of nowhere, Kathryn Kuhlman appeared. In an instant, the atmosphere in that building became charged. I didn't know what to expect. I didn't feel anything around me. No voices. No heavenly angels singing. Nothing. All I knew was that I had been shaking for three hours.

Then, as the singing began, I found myself doing something I never expected. I was on my feet. My hands were lifted, and tears streamed down my face as we sang "How Great Thou Art."

It was as if I had exploded. Never before had tears gushed from my eyes so quickly. Talk about ecstasy! It was a feeling of intense glory.

I wasn't singing the way I normally sang in church. I sang with my entire being. And when we came to the words, "Then sings my soul, my Savior God, to thee," I literally sang it from my soul.

I was so lost in the Spirit of that song that it took a few moments for me to realize that my shaking had completely stopped.

But the atmosphere of that service continued. I thought I had been totally raptured. I was worshiping beyond anything I had ever experienced. It was like coming face to face with pure spiritual truth. Whether anyone else felt it or not, I did.

In my young Christian experience, God had touched my life, but never as He was touching me that day.

Like a Wave

As I stood there, continuing to worship the Lord, I opened my eyes to look around because suddenly I felt a draft. And I didn't know where it was coming from. It was gentle and slow, like a breeze.

I looked at the stained-glass windows. But they were all closed. And they were much too high to allow such a draft.

The unusual breeze I felt, however, was more like a wave. I felt it go down one arm and up the other. I actually felt it moving.

What was happening? Could I ever have the courage to tell anyone what I felt? They would think I'd lost my mind.

For what seemed like ten minutes, the waves of that wind continued to wash over me. And then I felt as if someone had wrapped my body in a pure blanket—a blanket of warmth.

Kathryn began ministering to the people, but I was so lost in the Spirit that it really didn't matter. The Lord was closer to me than He had ever been.

I felt I needed to talk to the Lord, but all I could whisper was, "Dear Jesus, please have mercy on me." I said it again, "Jesus, please have mercy on me."

I felt so unworthy.

I felt like Isaiah when he entered the presence of the Lord.

> Woe is me, for I am undone!
> Because I am a man of unclean lips,
> And I dwell in the midst of a people of unclean lips;
> For my eyes have seen the King,
> The LORD of hosts. (Isa. 6:5)

The same thing happened when people saw Christ. They immediately saw their own filth, their need of cleansing.

That is what happened to me. It was as if a giant spotlight was beaming down on me. All I could see were my weaknesses, my faults, and my sins.

Again and again I said, "Dear Jesus, please have mercy on me."

Then I heard a voice that I knew must be the Lord. It was ever so gentle, but it was unmistakable. He said to me, "My mercy is abundant on you."

My prayer life to that point was that of a normal, average Christian. But now I was not just talking to the Lord. He was talking to me. And oh, what a communion that was!

Little did I realize that what was happening to me in the third row of the First Presbyterian Church in Pittsburgh was just a foretaste of what God had planned for the future.

Those words rang on in my ears. "My mercy is abundant on you."

I sat down crying and sobbing. There was just nothing in my life to compare with what I felt. I was so filled and transformed by the Spirit that nothing else mattered. I didn't care if a nuclear bomb hit Pittsburgh and the whole world blew up. At that moment I felt, as the Word describes it, "peace . . . which surpasses all understanding" (Phil. 4:7).

Jim had told me about the miracles that took place in Miss Kuhlman's meetings. But I had no idea what I was about to witness in the next three hours. People who were deaf suddenly could hear. A woman got up out of her wheelchair. There were testimonies of healings for tumors, arthritis, headaches, and more. Even her severest critics have acknowledged the genuine healings that took place in her meetings.

The service was long, but it seemed like a fleeting moment. Never in my life had I been so moved and touched by God's power.

Why Was She Sobbing?

As the service continued and I quietly prayed, everything stopped suddenly. I thought, "Please, Lord, don't ever let this meeting end."

I looked up to see Kathryn burying her head in her hands as she began to sob. She sobbed and sobbed so loudly that everything came to a standstill. The music stopped. The ushers froze in their positions.

Everyone had their eyes on her. And for the life of me I had no idea why she was sobbing. I'd never seen a minister do that before. What was she crying about? (I was told later that she had never done anything like that before, and members of her staff remember it to this day.)

It continued for what seemed like two minutes. Then she thrust back her head. There she was, just a few feet in front of me. Her eyes were aflame. She was *alive.*

In that instant she took on a boldness I had never seen in any person. She pointed her finger straight out with enormous power and emotion—even pain. If the devil himself had been there, she would have flicked him aside with just a tap.

It was a moment of incredible dimension. Still sobbing, she looked out at the audience and said with such agony, "Please." She seemed to stretch out the word, "Plee-ease, *don't grieve the Holy Spirit."*

She was begging. If you can imagine a mother pleading with a killer not to shoot her baby, it was like that. She begged and pleaded.

"Please," she sobbed, "don't grieve the Holy Spirit."

Even now I can see her eyes. It was as if they were looking straight at me.

And when she said it, you could have dropped a pin and heard it. I was afraid to breathe. I didn't move a muscle. I was holding on to the pew in front of me wondering what would happen next.

Then she said, *"Don't you understand? He's all I've got!"*

I thought, "What's she talking about?"

Then she continued her impassioned plea saying, "Please! Don't wound Him. He's all I've got. Don't wound the One I love!"

I'll never forget those words. I can still remember the intensity of her breathing when she said them.

In my church the pastor talked about the Holy Spirit. But not like this. His references had to do with the gifts or tongues or prophecy—not "He's my closest, most personal, most intimate, most beloved friend." Kathryn Kuhlman was telling me about a person that was more real than you or I.

Then she pointed her long finger down at me and said with great clarity, "He's more real than anything in this world!"

I've Got to Have It

When she looked at me and uttered those words, something literally grabbed me on the inside. It really got to me. I cried and said, "I've got to have this."

Now, frankly, I thought that everyone in that service would feel exactly the same way. But God has a way of dealing with us as individuals, and I believe that service was just for me.

Please understand, as a rather new Christian I couldn't begin to comprehend what was happening in that service. But I could not deny the reality and the power I felt.

And as the service came to a conclusion, I looked up at the woman evangelist and saw what seemed to be a mist around her and over her. At first I thought my eyes were playing tricks on me. But there it was. And her face was shining like a light through that mist.

I don't for one moment believe that God was trying to glorify Miss Kuhlman. But I do believe He used that service to reveal His power to me.

When the service was dismissed, the crowd filed out, but I didn't want to move. I had come in racing, but now I just wanted to sit down and reflect on what had just happened.

What I had felt in that building was something my personal life did not offer me. I knew that when I returned to my home, the persecution would continue.

My own self-image was practically destroyed because of my speech impediment. Even when I was a child in Catholic schools, my stuttering left me isolated with almost no one to talk to.

Even after I became a Christian, I made very few friends. How could I meet new people when I could hardly communicate?

So I never wanted what I found in Pittsburgh to leave me. All I had in life was Jesus. And nothing else in life had much meaning. I had no real future. My family had practically turned their backs on me. Oh, I knew they loved me, but my decision to serve Christ had created a gulf that was exceedingly wide.

I just sat there. After all, who wants to go to hell after they've been to heaven?

But there was no choice. The bus was waiting and I had to go back. I paused at the back of the church for one last moment, thinking, *What did she mean? What was she saying when she talked about the Holy Spirit?*

All the way back to Toronto I kept thinking, *I don't know what she meant.* I even asked a few people on the bus. They couldn't tell me because they did not understand either.

Needless to say, when I arrived home, I was totally exhausted. What with lack of sleep, hours on the road, and a spiritual experience that was like an emotional roller coaster, my body was ready for a rest.

But I could not sleep. My body was weary to the bone, but my spirit was still stirring like a never-ending series of volcanoes erupting inside me.

Knowing God's Presence

Who Is Pulling Me?

As I lay on my bed, I felt as if someone was pulling me off the mattress and onto my knees. It was a strange sensation, but I felt it so strongly I couldn't resist.

There I was, in the darkness of that room, on my knees. God wasn't through with me yet, and I responded to His leading.

I knew what I wanted to say, but I didn't quite know how to ask for it. What I wanted was what that minister in Pittsburgh had. I thought, *I want what Kathryn Kuhlman's got.* I wanted it with every atom and fiber within me. I hungered for what she was talking about—even though I didn't understand it.

Yes, I knew what I wanted to say but didn't know how to say it. So I decided to ask the only way I knew—in my own simple words.

I wanted to address the Holy Spirit, but I had never done that before. I thought, *Am I doing this right?* After all, I'd never spoken to the Holy Spirit. I never thought He was a person to be addressed. I didn't know how to start the prayer, but I knew what was inside me. All I wanted was to know Him the way she knew Him.

And here is what I prayed: "Holy Spirit. Kathryn Kuhlman says you are her friend." I slowly continued, "I don't think I know you. Now, before today I thought I did. But after that meeting I realize I really don't. I don't think I know you."

And then, like a child, with my hands raised, I asked, "Can I meet you? Can I really meet you?"

I wondered, *Is what I'm saying right? Should I be speaking to the Holy Spirit like this?* Then I thought, *If I'm honest in this, God will show me whether I'm right or wrong.* If Kathryn was wrong, I wanted to find out.

After I spoke to the Holy Spirit, nothing seemed to happen. I began to question myself, "Is there really such an experience as meeting the Holy Spirit? Can it truly happen?"

My eyes were closed. Then, like a jolt of electricity, my body began to vibrate all over—exactly as it had through the two hours I waited to get into the church. It was the same shaking I had felt for another hour once inside.

It was back, and I thought, *Oh. It's happening again.* But this time there were no crowds. No heavy clothes. I was just in my own warm room in my pajamas—vibrating from my head to my toes.

I was afraid to open my eyes. This time it was as if everything that happened in that service all rolled into one moment. I was shaking, but at the same time I again felt that warm blanket of God's power wrapped all around me.

I felt as if I had been translated to heaven. Of course I wasn't, but I honestly don't believe heaven can be any greater than that. In fact, I thought, *If I open my eyes, I'll either be in Pittsburgh or inside the pearly gates.*

Well, after a time, I did open my eyes, and to my surprise I was right there in my same room. Same floor. Same pajamas. But I was still tingling with the power of God's Spirit.

When I finally dropped off to sleep that night, I still didn't realize what had begun in my life.

The First Words I Spoke

Early, very early, the next morning I was wide awake. And I couldn't wait to talk to my newfound friend.

Here were the first words out of my mouth: *"Good morning, Holy Spirit!"*

At the very moment I spoke those words, the glorious atmosphere returned to my room. This time, though, I was not vibrating or shaking. All I felt was the wrapping of His presence.

The second I said, "Good morning, Holy Spirit," I knew He was present with me in the room. Not only was I filled with the Spirit that morning, I also received a fresh infilling every time I spent time in prayer.

What I am talking about is *beyond* speaking in tongues. Yes, I *did* speak in a heavenly language, but it was much more than that. The Holy Spirit became real. He became my friend. He became my companion, my counselor.

The first thing I did that morning was to open the Bible. I wanted to be sure. And as I opened the Word, I knew He was there with me as if He was sitting down beside me. No, I did not see His face or His countenance. But I knew where He was. And I began to know His personality.

From that moment on the Bible took on a whole new dimension. I would say, "Holy Spirit, show it to me in the Word." I wanted to know why He had come, and He led me to these words: "We have received, not the spirit of the world, but the Spirit who is from God, that we might know the things that have been freely given to us by God" (1 Cor. 2:12).

When I asked why He wanted to be my friend, He led me to the words of Paul: "The grace of the Lord Jesus Christ, and the love of God, and the communion of the Holy Spirit be with you all" (2 Cor. 13:14).

The Bible became alive. I had never really understood the impact of those words, " 'Not by might nor by power, but by My Spirit,' says the LORD" (Zech. 4:6).

Over and over again, He confirmed in the Word what He was doing in my life. For more than eight hours that first day, then day after day, I grew to know Him more.

My prayer life began to change. "Now," I said, "Holy Spirit, since you know the Father so well, would you help me pray?" And when I began to pray, I came to the place where suddenly the Father was more real than He had ever been before. It was as if someone had opened a door and said, "Here He is."

My Teacher, My Guide

The reality of the fatherhood of God became clearer than I had ever known. It was not by reading a book. Or following a formula—A, B, C. It was just by asking the Holy Spirit to open the Word to me. And He did. ". . . as many as are led by the Spirit of God, these are sons of God. For you did not receive the spirit of bondage again to fear, but you received the Spirit of adoption by whom we cry out, 'Abba, Father' " (Rom. 8:14–15).

I began to comprehend everything Jesus said about the Holy Spirit. He was my comforter, my teacher, my guide.

I understood for the first time what Jesus meant when He told His disciples, "Follow Me." Then one day He said, "Don't follow Me—because where I'm going you can't go." He told them, "But the Holy Ghost, He will guide you. He will lead you on."

What was He doing? Christ was giving them another leader. Another one to follow.

My search of the Scriptures went on day after day for weeks—until all of my questions were answered. All that time I was getting to know the Holy Spirit better. And that communion has never stopped to this day. I realized He was right here with me. And my entire life has been transformed. I believe yours will be too.

Today as I rose, I said it again: "Good morning, Holy Spirit."

TWO

From Jaffa to the Ends
of the Earth

It was December 1952 in Jaffa, Israel.

Clemence Hinn, about to give birth to her second child, was in the hospital, gazing out the window of her maternity room at a beautiful sight. The deep blue waters of the Mediterranean were stretched to infinity. But the heart of this small woman of Armenian descent was troubled. She was torn with bitterness, fear, and shame.

Off in the distance she could see the black cluster of rocks in the sea, Andromeda's Rocks. Greek legend holds that the maiden Andromeda was chained to one of them when Perseus flew down on his winged horse, slew the sea monster, and rescued her.

Clemence wanted someone somehow to swoop down and save her from another year of humiliation and disgrace. She was a devout Greek Orthodox woman, but she didn't know much about the Lord. In that humble hospital room, however, she tried to make a bargain with Him.

As she stood by the window, her eyes pierced the sky, and she spoke from her heart: "God, I have only one request. If you'll give me a boy, I'll give him back to you."

She repeated it again, "Please, Lord. If you'll give me a boy, I'll give him back to you."

Jaffa

Six Beautiful Roses

The first child born to Costandi and Clemence Hinn was a lovely girl, named Rose. But in the stubborn culture of the Middle East—and especially in the Hinn ancestral tradition—the firstborn should have been a son and heir.

The family of Costandi, immigrants to Palestine from Greece, began to persecute Clemence for her failure to produce a boy. "After all," they chided, "all of your other sister-in-laws had boys." She was jeered at and mocked to tears, and she felt the embarrassment and shame in a marriage their parents had so carefully arranged.

Her eyes were still moist that evening as she fell asleep. And during the night she had a dream she still recalls. "I saw six roses—six beautiful roses in my hand," she says. "And I saw Jesus enter my room. He came to me and asked me for one of them. And I gave Him one rose."

As the dream continued, a short, slim young man with dark hair—she remembers every feature of his face—came over to her and wrapped her in a warm cloth.

When she awakened, she asked herself, "What does this dream mean? What can it be?"

The next day, December 3, 1952, I was born.

Our family was eventually to have six boys and two girls, but my mother never forgot her bargain with God. She later told me of her dream—and that I was the rose she presented to Jesus.

I was christened in the Greek Orthodox Church by the patriarch of Jerusalem, Benedictus. In fact, during the ceremony he gave me his name.

Being born in the Holy Land meant being born in an atmosphere where religion casts an inescapably wide shadow. At the age of two I was enrolled in a Catholic preschool and was formally trained by nuns—and later monks—for fourteen years.

To me, Jaffa was a beautiful city. In fact, that is what the word itself means—beautiful. Jaffa in Arabic, Joppa in ancient Greek, or Yafo in Hebrew. In every language the meaning is the same.

As a boy I loved hearing the stories of history that surrounded me. Jaffa was founded back before recorded time. It is mentioned as a Canaanite city in the tribute lists of Pharaoh Thutmose III in the fifteenth century B.C., even before Joshua fought the battle of Jericho. And it is where the Phoenician King Hiram of Tyre unloaded cedar logs for King Solomon's temple.

Though it was fascinating, history had not been kind to my birthplace. Jaffa was invaded, captured, destroyed, and rebuilt again and again. Simon the Maccabee, Vespasian, the Mamelukes, Napoleon, and Allenby have all claimed her.

Only six years before I was born, Jaffa found herself in a new nation, the prophetic state of Israel. But the community itself was not Jewish.

Mayor Hinn

My father was the mayor of Jaffa during my childhood. He was a strong man, about 6'2", 250 pounds, and a natural leader. He was strong in every way—physically, mentally, and in will.

His family came from Greece to Egypt before settling in Palestine. But being "from somewhere else" was common. The Jaffa of my childhood was truly an international city.

Walking down Raziel Street into Tower Square that contains the Abdul Hamid Jubilee Clock Tower, the stone-walled jail, and the Great Mosque, built in 1810, I could hear locals conversing in French, Bulgarian, Arabic, Yiddish, and other languages. And in the kiosks and open-air cafes, I could sample baklava, zlabiya, felafel, sum-sum, and dozens of other delights.

So here I was, born in Israel, but not Jewish. Raised in an Arabic culture, but not of Arabic origin. Attending a Catholic school, but raised as a Greek Orthodox.

Languages come easy in that part of the world. I thought everyone was supposed to speak three or four. Arabic was spoken in our home, but at school the Catholic sisters taught in French, except for the Old Testament, which was studied in ancient Hebrew.

During my childhood, the hundred thousand people of Jaffa had become engulfed by the exploding Jewish population of Tel Aviv to the north. Today the metropolis has the official name of Tel Aviv-Jaffa. Over four hundred thousand live in the area.

Actually, Tel Aviv began as a Jewish experiment in 1909 when sixty families bought thirty-two acres of bare sand dunes just north of Jaffa and marched out to the site. They were tired of the cramped conditions and noisy Arab quarters where they lived. The expansion continued until Tel Aviv became Israel's largest city.

Even though my father was not Jewish, the Israeli leaders trusted him. And they were happy to have someone in Jaffa who could relate to such an international community. We were proud of his circle of friends, which included many national leaders. He was asked to be an ambassador for Israel in foreign nations, but chose to stay in Jaffa.

But there was little time for the family. In fact, I can't really say that I knew my father then. It seemed he was always attending an official function or an important meeting.

He wasn't a demonstrative person, just strict—and he seldom

showed any physical signs of affection. (My mother, however, made up for that.) Again, part of that was the culture. Men were men!

We lived comfortably. Dad's position in government made it possible for us to have a home in the suburbs. It was a wonderful home that had a wall around it with glass along the top for security. My mother was a homemaker in every sense of the word; raising that brood of little Hinns was more than a full-time job.

A Catholic Cocoon

As my education continued, I considered myself to be a Catholic. The process started very early. The preschool I attended was actually more like a convent. Mass was celebrated regularly. My parents didn't protest because a private Catholic school education was considered to be the best available.

Weekdays I studied with the nuns, and on Sunday I went to the Greek Orthodox church with Mom and Dad. But that was not considered a major problem in polyglot Jaffa. Loyalty to one particular church did not seem that important.

Was I a Catholic? Absolutely. Catholicism was my prayer life. It occupied my time and attention five days a week. It became my mentality. I practically lived at the convent, and in that cocoon I became very detached from the world.

I was also separated from the world in an unfortunate way. From earliest childhood I was afflicted with a severe stutter. The smallest amount of social pressure or nervousness triggered my stammering, and it was almost unbearable. I found it difficult to make friends. Some children made fun of me—others just stayed away.

I knew very little of world events—only what my teachers wanted me to know. But I was an expert on the Catholic life. As the schooling continued, I attended the College de Frere (College of Brothers) and was taught by monks.

Even as a small boy, I was extremely religious. I prayed and I prayed—probably more than some Christians pray today. But all I knew how to pray was the Hail Mary, the Creed, the Lord's Prayer, and other prescribed prayers.

Only rarely did I really talk to the Lord. When I had some specific request, I mentioned it. Otherwise my prayer life was all very organized. Very routine.

The one maxim seemed to be, "You should feel pain when you pray." And that was easy. There was practically nowhere to kneel except on the white Jerusalem rock that was everywhere. Most of the homes are made of it. And the schools I attended had no carpet, just plain white rock floors.

I actually came to believe that if you didn't suffer with your supplication, the Lord wouldn't hear you, that suffering was the best way to gain God's favor.

Even though virtually no spirituality accompanied the teaching, I still cherish the foundation I received in the Bible. I often think, *How many kids are taught the Old Testament in Hebrew?* And our field trips literally made God's Word come to life.

Once we traveled into the Negev where we stood next to the wells Abraham had dug and learned about him. That experience will stay with me forever.

His Robe Was Whiter Than White

Several times in my life God has spoken to me in a vision. It happened only once during my years in Jaffa, when I was just a boy of eleven.

I really believe it was at that moment that God began moving in my life. I can remember the vision as if it happened yesterday. I saw Jesus walk into my bedroom. He was wearing a robe that was whiter than white and a deep red mantle was draped over the robe.

I saw His hair. I looked into His eyes. I saw the nailprints in His hands. I saw everything.

You must understand that I did not know Jesus. I had not asked Christ to come into my heart. But the moment I saw Him, I recognized Him. I knew it was the Lord.

When it happened, I was asleep, but suddenly my little body was caught up in an incredible sensation that can only be described as "electric." It felt as if someone had plugged me into a wired socket. There was a numbness that felt like needles—a million of them—rushing through my body.

And then the Lord stood before me while I was in a deep, deep sleep. He looked straight at me with the most beautiful eyes. He smiled, and His arms were open wide. I could feel His presence. It was marvelous and I'll never forget it.

The Lord didn't say anything to me. He just looked at me. And then He disappeared.

Immediately I was wide awake. At the time I could scarcely understand what was happening, but it wasn't a dream. Those kinds of feelings don't happen in a dream. God allowed me to experience a vision that would create an indelible impression on my young life.

As I awakened, the wondrous sensation was still there. I opened my eyes and looked all around, but this intense, powerful feeling was still in me. I felt totally paralyzed. I couldn't move a muscle. Not an eyelash. I was completely frozen there. Yet I was in control. This unusual feeling overtook me—but didn't dominate me.

In fact, I felt I could say, "No, I don't want this," and the experience would have lifted. But I didn't say anything. While I lay there, awake, the feeling stayed with me, then slowly went away.

In the morning I told my mother about the experience, and she still remembers her words. She said, "You must be a saint, then."

Things like that didn't happen to people in Jaffa, whether they were Catholic or Greek Orthodox. Of course, I was certainly no "saint," but my mother believed that if Jesus came to me, He must be singling me out for a higher calling.

While God was dealing with my life, other factors were at work that would forever change the future of our family.

The Ends of the Earth

From Gaza to the Golan Heights

Living in Israel during the sixties, I could feel the escalating political tension. Arab raids into Israel occurred almost daily along the borders from Egypt to Jordan and Syria. And the Israeli army regularly retaliated with raids of their own.

In May 1967 Israel and the three Arab countries all alerted their armed forces for a possible war. At Egypt's demand the United Nations troops left the Gaza Strip and the Sinai Peninsula.

Then, on June 5, 1967, Israeli planes attacked airfields in Egypt, Jordan, and Syria. It was called the Six-Day War. In less than one week, the Israelis destroyed the Arab air forces almost completely. Israeli troops occupied the Gaza Strip, the Sinai Peninsula, the West Bank, and Syria's Golan Heights. Suddenly, Israel controlled Arab territory totaling more than three times the area of Israel itself.

I'll never forget the day, early in 1968, that my father gathered the family together and told us that he was making plans for us to emigrate. He said, "Please don't discuss it with anyone because there may be some problems with our exit visas."

In the beginning, the plan was to move to Belgium. Father had some relatives there, and the thought of moving to a French-speaking country sounded exciting. After all, that was the language of my schooling.

Then one evening an attaché from the Canadian embassy came

to our home and showed us a short movie on life in Canada. Toronto seemed like such a thriving city. Father had two brothers who lived there, but we doubted that they were financially qualified to be our official sponsor.

The questions surrounding our leaving seemed to grow day by day. At one point my father told us we might not be ready to depart the country for five years.

I Bargained with God

By that time we were all so anxious to leave that I got down on my knees—on that Jerusalem rock—and made a vow to God. "Lord," I prayed, "if You will get us out, I'll bring You the biggest jar of olive oil I can find." And I added, "When we get to Toronto, I'll bring it to church and present it to You in thanksgiving."

In my upbringing, bargaining with God wasn't unusual. And olive oil was a precious commodity. So I made the vow.

Within weeks a young man from the Canadian embassy called my father to say, "Mister Hinn. We've worked everything out—don't ask me how. All of your paperwork is in order, and you can leave whenever you're ready."

It didn't take long. We sold almost all our possessions and prepared for a new life in North America.

During those last days in the Holy Land, I had a keen sense that something great was about to happen. I knew I was leaving a special city, but I felt that the best was yet before me.

It was from the harbor of the ancient city of Joppa—my Jaffa—that Jonah left. And the result was the salvation of Nineveh.

And how many times had I climbed to the Citadel, the high mount overlooking the harbor. Near the lighthouse is a Franciscan church built in 1654. Next to it is the site of the house of Simon the Tanner where the apostle Peter stayed for some time and had a vision that changed the world. Hearing the voice of God telling him to receive Gentiles as well as Jews into the church, Peter responded, "In truth I perceive that God shows no partiality. But in every nation whoever fears Him and works righteousness is accepted by Him" (Acts 10:34–35).

From that very moment, the message of Christ was spread from Joppa to Caesarea and on to the ends of the earth—touching all of humankind.

As we drove down Haganah Road to the Lod airport, I wondered, *Will I ever see this place again?* I thought about those Catholic nuns who so lovingly had taught me. Had I seen their faces for the last time?

Out of the plane window I took one last look down at Tel Aviv, a huge expanse of gray-white cubes. Behind me were miles of deep green orange groves. The Judean hills gleamed faintly in the distance.

And as we headed over the waters of the Mediterranean, I looked down and said one last good-bye to Jaffa. There was a lump in my throat. I was fourteen, and it was the only home I had ever known.

Ice Cream at the Kiosk

The Hinn family arrival in Toronto in July 1968 was an unheralded event. And that's just the way my father wanted it. No welcoming committee met us. And he had no promise of a job.

We arrived with the clothes on our backs, a few possessions in suitcases, and a little money from what we had sold in Jaffa. It was enough to get by for a short time.

Our new life began in a rented apartment.

What a shock to land suddenly in a "foreign" culture. I could stutter in several languages, but English was not one of them. "One, two, three," was as far as it went. But Daddy had studied enough

English to fill out a job application. And it worked. He accepted the challenge of becoming, of all things, an insurance salesman.

I don't know whether it was the burden of having to raise a large family, or his natural confidence in dealing with people, but my dad became an immediate success in his newfound profession. And before too many months we moved into our own home. We were all so proud of it.

Life changed rapidly for me. Instead of attending a private Catholic school, I went to a public high school—Georges Vanier Secondary School. And since most of the kids at school had part-time jobs, that's what I wanted to do.

We lived in the North York section of Toronto, and not far from us the new Fairview Mall had opened. I applied at a little kiosk that sold hamburgers and ice cream. Even though I had no previous work experience, they hired me. And every day after school I headed there.

One Saturday, though, I walked into a grocery store and asked the manager, "Where can I find the olive oil? I need the largest jug or container of it you have." Sure enough, he found a big one.

The next day, I walked proudly into the Greek Orthodox church and made good on my vow to God. I placed it at the front of the altar and quietly said, "Thank you, Lord. Thank you for bringing us safely to our new home."

My heart was as full as that jug of oil.

At the kiosk I did my work. Because of my stutter, I didn't get into many conversations, but I did become a whiz at packing the ice cream into those sugar cones. I worked with a fellow named Bob.

Had Bob Lost His Mind?

I'll never forget the day in 1970 when I came to work to find that Bob had done something quite strange. All over the walls of that little kiosk he had tacked little pieces of paper with Scripture verses written on them. I thought he'd lost his mind.

I knew he was a Christian—he told me so. But wasn't this going a bit too far? I said to myself, "Why is he doing this? Is it for me? I probably know the Bible better than he does."

Finally I asked him, "What's the idea of all these pieces of paper?" Instantly, he began to witness to me. I thought he would never quit. And when it was over, I was determined to stay as far away from this crazy fellow as I could.

For the longest time I tried to avoid him. But it was nearly impossible. After all, we had to work together. Over and over, he brought up the topic of religion. But it was more than that. He wanted to talk about being "born again," a phrase that was not in my limited vocabulary—not in my view of Scripture.

Bob finally quit his job at the kiosk, but many of his friends were at my school. And for the next two years I did my best to avoid them. I thought, *They're a bunch of weirdos.* They looked weird. They talked weird. They were complete opposites of the nuns who had taught me.

During my senior year at Georges Vanier, for the second time in my life I had an encounter with the Lord. He came into my room and visited me—this time in the form of an unforgettable dream.

In Jaffa when I was eleven, the vision of Jesus standing before me had left an indelible impression. But now, in Toronto, I was not caught up in the study of Scripture. Oh, I still attended church. But what was about to happen to me came out of left field. It was totally unexpected, and I was stunned by the experience.

Let me tell you exactly what happened in my bedroom that chilly night in February 1972.

As the dream unfolded, I found myself descending a long, dark stairway. It was so steep I thought I would fall. And it was leading me into a deep, endless chasm.

I was bound by a chain to a prisoner in front of me and a prisoner behind me. I was dressed in the clothing of a convict. There were chains on my feet and around my wrists. As far as I could see ahead of me and behind me there was a never-ending line of captives.

Then, in the eerie haze of that dimly lit shaft, I saw dozens of small people moving around. They were like imps with strange-shaped ears. I couldn't see their faces, and their forms were barely visible. But we were obviously being pulled down the stairway by them, like a herd of cattle to a slaughterhouse—or even worse.

Suddenly, appearing out of nowhere, was the angel of the Lord. Oh, it was a wondrous thing to behold. The heavenly being hovered just ahead of me, just a few steps away.

Never in my life had I seen such a sight—not even in a dream. A bright and beautiful angel in the midst of that dark, black hole.

As I looked again, the angel motioned with his hand for me to come to him. Then he looked into my eyes and called me out. My eyes were riveted to his, and I began to walk toward him. Instantly those bonds fell off my hands and feet. I was no longer tied to my fellow prisoners.

Hurriedly the angel led me through an open doorway, and the moment I walked into the light, the celestial being took me by the hand and dropped me on Don Mills Road—right at the corner of Georges Vanier School. He left me just inches from the wall of the school, right beside a window.

In a second the angel was gone, and I woke up early and rushed off to school to study in the library before classes began.

"I Could Hardly Blink"

As I sat there, not even thinking about the dream, a small group of students walked over to my table. I recognized them immediately. They were the ones who had been pestering me with all of this "Jesus" talk.

They asked me to join in their morning prayer meeting. The room was just off the library. I thought, "Well, I'll get them off my back. One little prayer meeting isn't going to hurt me."

I said, "All right," and they walked with me into the room. It was a small group, just twelve or fifteen kids. And my chair was right in the middle.

All of a sudden the entire group lifted their hands and began to pray in some funny foreign language. I didn't even close my eyes. I could hardly blink. Here were students seventeen, eighteen, nineteen years old—kids I had known in class—praising God with unintelligible sounds.

I had never heard of speaking in tongues, and I was dumbfounded. To think that here was Benny, in a public school, on public property, sitting in the middle of a bunch of babbling fanatics. It was almost more than I could comprehend.

I didn't pray. I just watched.

What happened next was more than I could ever have imagined. I was startled by a sudden urge to pray. But I really didn't know what to say. "Hail Mary," seemed inappropriate for what I was feeling. I had never been taught the "sinner's prayer"—not in all of my religion classes. All I could remember of my encounters with the "Jesus people" was the phrase, "You've got to meet Jesus." Those words seemed out of place to me because I thought I knew Him.

It was an awkward moment. No one was praying with me or even *for* me. Yet I was surrounded by the most intense spiritual atmosphere I had ever felt. Was I a sinner? I didn't think so. I was just a good little Catholic boy, who prayed every night and confessed sin whether I needed to or not.

But at that moment I closed my eyes and said four words that changed my life forever. Right out loud I said, "Lord Jesus, come back."

I don't know why I said it, but that's all that would come out of my mouth. I repeated those words again and again. "Lord Jesus, come back. Lord Jesus, come back."

Did I think He had left my house or departed from my life? I really did not know. But the moment I uttered those words a feeling came over me—it took me back to the numbness I felt at age eleven. It was less intense, but I could feel the voltage of that same force. It went right through me.

What I really felt, though, was that this surge of power was cleansing me—instantly, from the inside out. I felt absolutely clean, immaculate, and pure.

Suddenly I saw Jesus with my own eyes. It happened in a moment of time. There He was. Jesus.

Five Minutes to Eight

The students around me couldn't possibly know what was taking place in my life. They were all praying. Then, one by one, they began slipping out of the room and on to their classes.

It was five minutes to eight o'clock in the morning. By this time I was just sitting there crying. I didn't know what to do or what to say.

At the time I didn't understand it, but Jesus became as real to me as the floor beneath my feet. I didn't really pray, except for those four words. But I knew beyond any doubt that something extraordinary had happened that February morning.

I was almost late for history. It was one of my favorite subjects;

we were studying the Chinese Revolution. But I couldn't even hear the teacher. I don't remember anything that was said. The feeling that began that morning would not leave me. Every time I closed my eyes, there He was—Jesus. And when I opened my eyes, He was still there. The picture of the Lord's face would not leave me.

All day I was wiping the tears from my eyes. And the only thing I could say was, "Jesus, I love you. . . . Jesus, I love you."

As I walked out of the door of the school and down the sidewalk to the corner, I looked at the window of the library. And the pieces began to fall into place.

The angel. The dream. It all became real again.

What was God trying to tell me?

What was happening to Benny?

THREE

"Tradition, Tradition"

I walked into my bedroom, and, as if magnetized, I was drawn to that big black Bible. It was the only Bible in our home. Mom and Dad didn't even have one. I had no idea where it came from, but it had been mine as long as I could remember.

The pages had hardly been turned since our arrival in Canada, but now I prayed, "Lord, You've got to show me what has happened to me today." I opened the Scripture and began to devour it like a starving man who has just been given a loaf of bread.

The Holy Spirit became my teacher. I didn't know it at the time, but that's exactly what miraculously began to happen. You see, the kids at the prayer meeting didn't say, "Now here's what the Bible says." They didn't tell me anything. In fact, they had no idea what had transpired during the past twenty-four hours. And, of course, I didn't say a word to my parents.

I began by reading the Gospels. I found myself saying out loud, "Jesus, come into my heart. Please, Lord Jesus, come into my heart."

In Scripture after Scripture I saw the plan of salvation unfolding. It was as if I had never read the Bible before. Oh, my friend, it was alive. The words bubbled forth from a spring, and I drank freely from it.

Finally, at three or four o'clock in the morning, with a quiet peace that I had never known before, I fell asleep.

Belonging

The next day at school I sought out those "fanatics" and said, "Hey, I'd like you to take me to your church." They told me about a weekly fellowship they attended and offered to take me just a couple of days later.

That Thursday night I found myself in "The Catacombs." That's what they called it. The service was just like that morning prayer meeting at school—people had their hands lifted, worshiping the Lord. This time, though, I joined right in.

"Jehovah Jireh, my provider, His grace is sufficient for me," they sang over and over. I liked that song from the first time I heard it and loved it even more when I found out it was written by the pastor's wife, Merla Watson. Her husband, Merv, was the shepherd of this most unusual flock.

The Catacombs was not a typical church. The people who went there were just an exuberant throng of Christians that met every Thursday night in St. Paul's Cathedral, an Anglican church in downtown Toronto.

These were "Jesus Movement" days when the so-called "hippies" were getting saved faster than they could cut their hair. Come to think of it, I hadn't seen a barber's chair either in quite some time.

I looked around. The place was packed with kids just like me. You should have seen it. They were jumping up and down, dancing and making a joyful noise before the Lord. It was hard for me to believe that a place like that really existed. But somehow, from that very first night, I felt I belonged.

"Go Up There"

At the conclusion of the meeting, Merv Watson said, "I want all of you who would like to make a public confession of our sin to step forward. We're going to pray with you as you ask Christ to come into your heart."

I began to shiver and shake. But I thought, *I don't think I should go down there because I'm already saved.* I knew the Lord took charge of my life at five minutes to eight on Monday morning. And this was Thursday.

You guessed it. Within seconds I found myself walking down that aisle as fast as I could. I didn't quite know why I did it. But something inside was telling me, "Go up there."

It was at that moment, at a charismatic service in an Anglican church, that this good little Catholic from a Greek Orthodox home made a public confession of his acceptance of Christ. "Jesus," I said, "I'm asking You to be the Lord of my life."

The Holy Land couldn't compare with this. How much better to be where Jesus *was*, than where He used to be.

That night when I got home, I was so filled with the presence of the Lord. I decided to tell my mother what had happened. (I didn't have the courage to tell my dad.)

"Mama, I've got to share something with you," I whispered. "I've been saved!"

In a flash, her jaw was set. She glared and said crisply, "Saved from what?"

"Trust me," I said. "You'll understand."

On Friday morning and all during the day—at school, at the kiosk, everywhere I went, a picture kept flashing before me. I saw myself preaching. It was unthinkable, but I couldn't shake the image. I saw crowds of people. And there I was, wearing a suit, my hair all trimmed and neat, preaching up a storm.

That day I found Bob, my "weird" friend who had once plastered the kiosk walls with Scripture. I shared just a little about what had happened that week. And I told him that I even saw myself preaching.

"Bob," I said, "all day long it's been like this. I can't shake the picture of me speaking in huge open-air rallies, in stadiums, in churches, in concert halls." Beginning to stutter, I told him, "I see people, as far as the eye can see! I must be losing my mind! What do you think it means?"

"There can only be one thing," he told me. "God is preparing you for a great ministry. I think it's wonderful."

Cast Out

I didn't get that kind of encouragement at home. Of course, I really couldn't tell them what the Lord was doing.

The situation was dreadful.

Humiliation and Shame

My entire family began to harass and ridicule me. It was horrible. I expected it from my father, but not my mother. When I was growing up, she had showed so much affection. So had my brothers and sisters. But now they treated me with disdain—like an intruder who didn't belong.

"Tradition! Tradition!" says the song in *Fiddler on the Roof.* If an Easterner breaks tradition, he has committed an unpardonable sin. I doubt that the West will ever truly understand its seriousness. He brings humiliation upon his family. And that can't be forgiven.

The family told me, "Benny, you're ruining our family name." They pleaded with me not to dishonor their reputation. My father had been a mayor—and he reminded me of it. The family "name" was at stake.

Please understand me when I say this, but Greek Orthodox, and people from other Eastern "high" church orders are perhaps the most difficult people to bring to a "personal" Christianity.

When I became a born-again Christian, it was actually shameful to them. Why? Because they believe they are the *real* Christians. And they have the historical documentation to prove it. They have been Christians longer than anyone else.

But here is the problem, and I have been raised with it. Their faith is long on form, ritual, and dogma, but short on God's anointing. The power is missing. And as a result, they have virtually no comprehension of what it means to hear from the Lord or to be "led by the Spirit."

It became obvious that if I was to remain in my own home, I would have to close the door to conversations about Christ.

Nothing, however, could dampen the fire of my newfound faith. I was like a glowing ember that never stopped burning.

Early in the morning my big Bible was open. The Holy Spirit continued to reveal the Word. But that was not enough. Every night that I could "escape" the house, I was in a church service, youth fellowship, or prayer meeting. And on Thursday nights I was back at The Catacombs.

I can never erase from my memory the day I mentioned "Jesus" in our home. My father walked over to me and slapped my face. I felt the pain. No, it wasn't the Jerusalem rock this time. It was a different kind of pain. But the hurt I felt was for my family. I loved them so much and agonized for their salvation.

Actually, it was my fault. My daddy had warned me, "You

mention the name of Jesus just once again, and you'll wish you hadn't." He snarled with hatred as he threatened to kick me out of the house.

I began to tell my little sister, Mary, about the Lord. Somehow my dad found out about it, and his anger boiled over again. He forbade me to ever talk to her about spiritual things.

Time for the Psychiatrist

Even my brothers persecuted me. They called me every name under heaven—and a few below the earth. It went on for such a long time. In my room I prayed, "Lord, will it ever end? Will they ever come to know You?"

It got to a place where there wasn't a member of my family I could talk to. I didn't have to look up the definition of *ostracized*.

They flew my grandmother over from Israel just to tell me I was crazy. "You are an embarrassment to the family name," she said. "Don't you understand the shame you're causing?"

My father made an appointment for me to see a psychiatrist. Evidently Dad thought I had lost my mind. And what was the doctor's conclusion? "Maybe your son is going through something. He'll come out of it."

His next tactic was to get me a job that would keep me so busy that I wouldn't have time for this "Jesus." He went to one of his friends and said, "I'd like for you to offer my son, Benny, a job."

Daddy drove me to his place and waited in the car while I went in. The man was one of the rudest, roughest, most mean-spirited men I had ever encountered. It was obvious I couldn't work for such a person.

I got back in the car and said, "Father, I could never have him for a boss."

I actually felt sorry for my dad that day. He was at the end of his rope. He said, "Benny, what do you want me to do for you? Tell me what it is. I'll do anything you ask if you'll just please leave this Jesus of yours."

"Dad," I said, "you can ask me anything you want, but I would die before I'd give up what I've found."

It was an ugly scene. He turned from a friendly father into a sarcastic stranger. All he had to offer was another torrent of hate, another tongue-lashing.

For the next year—nearly two—my father and I had almost no communication. At the dinner table he wouldn't look at me. I was totally ignored. It finally became unbearable even to sit down and watch the evening news with my family.

So what did I do? I stayed in my room. But looking back on it, I can see that the Lord knew exactly what He was doing. I spent hundreds of hours—thousands—alone with God. My Bible was always open. I prayed. I studied. I worshiped. I feasted on heavenly manna that I would need in the years to come.

"I Must Obey the Lord"

Getting to church was a gigantic problem. How I longed to go, but my father said, "Absolutely not!" time and time again. In fact, those were practically the only conversations we had—arguments about the house of the Lord.

Easterners consider it unthinkable to disobey parents. But now I was nearly twenty-one. And I vividly recall the night I summoned the boldness to tell my father, "I'll obey you on anything you want, but on the matter of going to church I will not obey you. *I must obey the Lord!*"

He was stunned. You'd have thought someone had shot him. And he seemed to bristle even more.

Out of respect, I did my best to be obedient. I'd ask him, "Can

I go to the meeting tonight?" He'd say no, and I would go to my room and pray, "Please, Lord, please change his mind."

Then I'd go back downstairs and ask again. "Can I go?" "No," he'd growl. And back up I'd go.

Little by little, he began to give in. He knew it was a losing battle. The Catacombs rented another building for services on Sunday, and I was right there. Bible studies were on Tuesday and Friday, and a youth meeting on Saturday night. These meetings became my whole life.

In the two years after my conversion, my spiritual growth was like a rocket's moving into orbit. By the end of 1973 Merv and Merla Watson were inviting me to join them on the platform to help lead in worship and singing. But I couldn't speak in public.

Jim Poynter, the spirit-filled Free Methodist pastor, had seen me there. And one day he stopped by the kiosk at the mall just to talk about the things of the Lord. That's when he invited me to go with him to the Kuhlman meeting in Pittsburgh.

My personal encounter with the Holy Spirit after that meeting was awesome. But it took a few days for me to realize the dimensions of God's revelation to me.

About this same time I changed jobs. I accepted a position as a filing clerk for the Catholic school board in Toronto. I'm sure they wondered about me at times. I had a smile on my face just thinking about what God was doing in my life.

The minute my work was finished, I went home and rushed upstairs and just started talking to Him. "Oh, Holy Spirit, I'm so glad to be back here alone with you." Yes, He was always with me, but my bedroom became a very sacred, special place. Sometimes, when I wasn't working I stayed home all day just having a personal communion with Him.

What was I doing? Having *fellowship*. Fellowship with the Spirit.

And when I wasn't at work or in my room, I tried to get to church. But I didn't tell anyone what was happening to me.

When I left the house in the morning, He left with me. I actually felt someone beside me. On a bus I'd feel the urge to start talking with Him, but I didn't want people to think I was crazy. Even at work, there were times when I whispered things to Him. At lunch, He was my companion. But day after day, when I got home, I hopped up those stairs, locked the door to my room, and said, "Now we are alone." And my spiritual journey continued.

Anointing in the Car

Let me explain that many times I wasn't aware of His presence. I knew He was with me, but I became so accustomed to Him that I did not feel the electricity of those special times.

But other people felt it. Many times when my friends came to see me, they began weeping because of the presence of the Holy Spirit.

Once Jim Poynter called to say, "I want to pick you up and take you to a Methodist church where I'm singing. You can sing with me if you'd like." I wasn't really a singer, but I helped him out once in a while.

That afternoon I was once again lost in the anointing of God's spirit. Then I heard Jim honking the horn. As I ran down the stairs and to the car, I actually felt the Lord's presence running with me.

The moment I jumped into the front seat and shut the door, Jim began to weep. He began to sing that chorus, "Hallelujah! Hallelujah!" He turned to me and said, "Benny, I can feel the Holy Spirit in this car."

"Of course His presence is in this car," I said. "Where else would it be?" To me it had become the norm. But Jim could hardly drive. He continued to weep before the Lord.

Once, my mother was cleaning the hallway while I was in my room talking with the Holy Spirit. When I came out, she was thrown right back. Something had knocked her against the wall. I said, "What's wrong with you, Mama?" She answered, "I don't know?" Well, the presence of the Lord almost knocked her down.

My brothers will tell you of the times they came near me and didn't know what was happening—but they felt something unusual.

As time went on I lost my desire just to go out with the young people at church to have fun. I just wanted to be with the Lord. So often I said, "Lord, I'd rather have this than anything the world can offer." They could have their games, their entertainment, their football—I just didn't need it.

"What I want is what I have right now," I told the Lord. "Whatever it is, don't let it quit." I began to understand more fully Paul's desire for "the fellowship of the Holy Spirit."

Henry, Mary, Sammy, and Willie

Now, even members of my family were asking questions. The Spirit of the Lord so permeated our home, that my brothers and sisters began to develop a spiritual hunger.

One by one, they came to me and began to ask questions. They'd say, "Benny, I've been watching you. This Jesus is real, isn't He?"

My sister Mary gave her heart to the Lord. And within the next few months my little brother Sammy got saved. Then came Willie.

All I could do was to shout, "Hallelujah!" It was happening—and I had not even begun to preach.

By this time my father was nearly ready for an asylum. Was he losing his whole family to this Jesus? He didn't know how to handle it. But there was no question that my mom and dad could see the transformation that had already taken place in me, in two of my brothers, and in Mary.

When I first gave my life to the Lord, I had some wonderful encounters with Him. But these were nothing compared with my daily walk with the Holy Spirit. Now the Lord *really* visited my room. The glory would fill that place. Some days I'd be on my knees worshiping the Lord for eight, nine, or ten hours straight.

The year of 1974 unleashed a never-ending flow of God's power on my life. I'd just say "Good morning, Holy Spirit," and it would start all over again. The glory of the Lord stayed with me.

One day in April I thought, *There must be a reason for it.* I asked, "Lord, why are You doing all of this for me?" I knew that God doesn't give people spiritual picnics forever.

Then as I began to pray, here is what God revealed to me. I saw someone standing in front of me. He was totally in flames, moving uncontrollably; his feet were not touching the ground. The mouth of this being was opening and closing—like what the Word describes as "gnashing of teeth."

At that moment the Lord spoke to me in an audible voice. He said, "Preach the gospel."

My response, of course, was, "But Lord, I can't talk."

Two nights later the Lord gave me a second dream. I saw an angel. He had a chain in his hand, attached to a door that seemed to fill the whole heaven. He pulled it open, and there were people as far as the eye could see. Souls. They were all moving toward a large, deep valley—and the valley was a roaring inferno of fire.

It was frightening. I saw thousands of people falling into that fire. Those on the front lines were trying to fight it, but the crush of humanity behind them pushed them into the flames.

Again, the Lord spoke to me. Very clearly He said, "If you do not preach, everyone who falls will be your responsibility." I knew instantly that everything that happened in my life was for one purpose—to preach the gospel.

It Happened in Oshawa

The fellowship continued. The glory continued. The presence of the Lord did not depart; it actually intensified. The Word became more real. My prayer life became more powerful.

Finally, in November 1974 I couldn't avoid the subject any longer. I said to the Lord, "I will preach the gospel on one condition: that you will be with me in every service." And then I reminded Him, "Lord, you know that I can't talk." I worried continually about my speech problem and the fact that I was going to embarrass myself.

It was impossible, however, to erase from my mind the picture of a burning man and the sound of the Lord saying, "If you do not preach, everyone who falls will be your responsibility."

I thought, "I must begin to preach." But wouldn't passing out little tracts be good enough? Then one afternoon, the first week of December, I was sitting in the home of Stan and Shirley Phillips in Oshawa, about thirty miles east of Toronto.

"Can I tell you something?" I asked. Never before had I felt led to tell anyone the full story about my experiences, dreams, and visions. For nearly three hours, I poured out my heart about things only the Lord and I knew about.

Before I had finished, Stanley stopped me and said, "Benny, tonight you must come to our church and share this." They had a fellowship called Shilo—about a hundred people at the Trinity Assembly of God in Oshawa.

I wish you could have seen me. My hair was down to my shoulders, and I hadn't dressed for church because the invitation had been totally unexpected.

But on December 7, 1974, Stan introduced me to the group, and for the first time in my life I stood behind a pulpit to preach. The instant I opened my mouth, I felt something touch my tongue and loosen it. It felt like a little numbness, and I began to proclaim God's Word with absolute fluency.

Here's what was amazing. God didn't heal me when I was sitting in the audience. He didn't heal me when I was walking up to the platform. He didn't heal me when I stood behind the pulpit. God performed the miracle when I opened my mouth.

When my tongue loosened, I said, "That's it!" The stuttering was gone. All of it. And it has never returned.

Now my parents didn't know I was healed because we had so little communication around the house. And, of course, there had always been times when I could speak without a noticeable problem for a short time—before something set the stuttering off again.

But I knew I was healed. And my ministry began to mushroom. It seemed as if every day I was invited to a church or fellowship group to minister. I felt in the perfect center of God's Will.

"I'm Going to Die"

For the next five months I was a preacher but my mother and father had no inkling. Keeping it quiet for so long was a miracle in itself. My brothers knew, but they didn't dare tell Dad because they knew it would be the end of Benny.

In the *Toronto Star* in April 1975, a newspaper ad with my picture in it appeared. I was preaching at a little pentecostal church on the west side of town, and the pastor wanted to attract some visitors.

It worked. Costandi and Clemence saw the ad.

I was sitting on the platform that Sunday night. During the song service I looked up and could hardly believe my eyes. There were my mother and my father being ushered to a seat just a few rows in front of the platform.

I thought, "This is it. I'm going to die."

My good friend Jim Poynter was seated on the platform next to me. I turned to him and said, "Pray, Jim! Pray!" He was shocked when I told him Mother and Dad were there.

A thousand thoughts flashed through my mind, not the least of which was, *Lord, I'll know I'm really healed if I don't stutter tonight.* I can't remember another time that I was so nervous during a service and anxiety always made me stutter.

As I began to preach, the power of God's presence began to flow through me, but I couldn't bring myself to look in the direction of my parents—not even for a fleeting glance. All I knew was that my concern about stuttering was needless. When God healed me, the healing was permanent.

Toward the end of the service I began praying for those who needed a healing. Oh, the power of God filled that place.

As the meeting was ending, my parents got up and walked out the back door.

After the service I said to Jim, "You've got to pray. Do you realize that in the next few hours my destiny will be decided? I may have to sleep at your house tonight."

That night I drove aimlessly around Toronto. I wanted to wait until at least two in the morning to get home. By that time I knew my parents would be in bed.

I really didn't want to face them.

But more about that later.

FOUR

Person to Person

A re you ready to meet the Holy Spirit intimately and personally? Do you want to hear His voice? Are you prepared to know Him as a *person*?

That's exactly what happened to me, and it drastically transformed my life. It was an intensely personal experience, and it was based on God's Word.

You may ask, "Was it the result of a systematic Bible study?" No, it happened when I invited the Holy Spirit to be my personal friend. To be my constant guide. To take me by the hand and lead me "into all truth." What *He* will uncover and reveal to you in Scripture will make your study of the Bible come alive.

What I am about to share with you began the moment the Holy Spirit entered my room in December 1973, and it has never stopped. Here is the only difference: *I know Him infinitely better today than I did when we first met.*

Let's start with the basics. The Holy Spirit changed my life. He was with me from the moment I asked Christ to come into my heart and became born again.

Then came the time when I received the baptism of the Holy Spirit. I was "filled" with the Spirit. I spoke in tongues. He imparted His presence and His gifts. So many Christians have received that same experience and stop right there. They fail to realize that what happened at pentecost was only *one* of the gifts of the Spirit.

But what I want you to know is this: beyond salvation, beyond being baptized in water, beyond the infilling of the Spirit, the "third Person of the Trinity" is waiting for you to meet Him personally. He yearns for a lifelong relationship. And that is what you are about to discover.

Drawn into Fellowship

If you had dialed my telephone number two years ago and we got acquainted by phone and if we had continued our conversations but had never met, what would you really know about me?

You say, "I'd know the sound of your voice as it comes through the phone." And that would be just about it. You wouldn't recognize me if you saw me on the street.

But then the day comes when we meet face to face. All of a sudden you reach out to shake my hand. You see what I look like, the color of my hair and eyes, what kind of clothes I wear. Perhaps we go out for a meal, and you learn whether I like coffee or tea.

You learn volumes about people when you meet them in person.

End of the Struggle

When the Holy Spirit and I met, that is what began to happen. I began to discover things about His personality that changed me as a Christian. Salvation transformed me as a person. But the Spirit had a tremendous effect on my Christian walk.

As I began to know the Holy Spirit, I became sensitive to Him and learned what grieves Him—and what pleases Him. What He likes, what He doesn't like. What gets Him angry and what makes Him happy.

I came to understand that the Bible itself was written by the Holy Spirit. He used men from all walks of life, but every one of them was led by the Spirit.

For so long I struggled to understand the Bible. Then came the day that I looked up and said, "Wonderful Holy Spirit. Would you please tell me what you mean by this?" And He spoke. He revealed the Word to me.

The Lord used a Kathryn Kuhlman meeting to prepare me for what was about to happen. But never once did Miss Kuhlman sit with me and tell me about the Holy Spirit. Everything I learned was from Him. And that's why it's fresh, why it's new, and why it's *mine*.

When I returned home from that meeting in Pittsburgh, I fell to my knees. I was honest and transparent when I said, "Precious Holy Spirit, I want to know you." I will never forget how nervous I was. But from that day I have grown to know Him like a brother. Truly, He is a member of the family.

Who He Is

You ask, "Who is the Holy Spirit?" I want you to know He is the most beautiful, most precious, loveliest person on the earth. God the Son is not on the earth. God the Father is not on the earth. They are both in heaven this very second.

Who is on earth? *God the Holy Spirit*. For God the Father came to do His work through the Son who was resurrected. When God the Son departed, God the Holy Spirit came, and He is still here doing His work.

Think about it. When God the Son left, He would not even take

John and Peter with Him. He said, "Little children, I shall be with you a little while longer. You will seek Me; and as I said to the Jews, 'Where I am going, you cannot come'. . ." (John 13:33).

But when God the Holy Spirit leaves, which many believe is going to happen very soon, He's going to take the redeemed of the Lord with Him. It is called the Rapture. We will be caught up with Him to meet the Lord in the air.

Who is this Holy Spirit? I thought at one time He was like a vapor, something floating around that I could never really know. I learned that He is not only real, but that He has a personality.

What's on the Inside?

What makes me a person? Is it my physical body? I think not. I'm sure you have been to a funeral and have seen a body lying in a casket. Are you looking at a person? No! You are looking at a dead body.

You must realize that what makes a person is not the body. Instead, the person is what comes out of the body. Emotions. Will. Intellect. Feelings. These are just a few of the characteristics that make you a person and give you a personality.

People who watch me preach are not looking at Benny Hinn. They are only seeing my body. I am inside my physical body. It is the person *inside* who is important.

The Holy Spirit is a person. And just like you, He can feel, perceive, and respond. He gets hurt. He has the ability to love and the ability to hate. He speaks, and He has His own will.

But exactly who is He? *The Holy Spirit is the Spirit of God the Father and the Spirit of God the Son.* He is the power of the Godhead—the power of the Trinity.

What is His job? The task of the Spirit is to bring into being the commandment of the Father and the performance of the Son.

To understand the job of the Holy Spirit we need to understand the work of the Father and the Son. *God the Father is the one who gives the command.* He has always been the one who says, "Let there be." From the beginning, it has been God who gives the orders.

On the other hand, *it is God the Son who performs the commands of the Father.* When God the Father said, "Let there be light," God the Son came and performed it. Then, God the Holy Spirit *brought* the light.

Let me illustrate it this way. If I asked you, "Please turn on the light," three forces would be involved. First, I would be the one who gave the command. Second, you would be the one who walks to the switch and flips it. In other words, you are the performer of the command. But finally, who brings on the light? It is not me, and it is not you. It is the power—the electricity—that produces light.

The Holy Spirit is the power of God. He is the power of the Father and of the Son. He is the one who brings into action the performance of the Son. Yet He is a person. He has emotions which are expressed in a way unique among the Trinity.

I've been asked, "Benny, aren't you forgetting the importance of Christ in all of this?" Never! How could I forget the One who loved and died for me? But some people are so focused on the Son that they forget the Father—the one who loved them and sent His Son. I cannot forget the Father nor the Son. But *I cannot be in touch with the Father and the Son without the Holy Spirit* (see Eph. 2:18).

Fellowship

During one of my first encounters with the Holy Spirit I had an experience that moved me to tears. Just as simply as I am talking to you, I asked Him, "What am I supposed to do with You? Would you please tell me what You're like?" Honestly, I was like a little child trying to learn. And I felt that He would not be angry with my honest questions.

The Fellowship Meeting

Here's the answer the Holy Spirit gave: "I am the one who fellowships with you." And like the snap of a finger, that verse flashed before me: "The grace of the Lord Jesus Christ, and the love of God, and the communion of the Holy Spirit be with you all" (2 Cor. 13:14).

I thought, *That's it! The Holy Spirit is the one who communes, who fellowships with me.* Then I asked, "How can I fellowship with You, but not with the Son?" And He responded, "That is exactly as it should be. I am here to help you in your prayers to the Father. And I am here to help you pray to the Son."

Immediately, my entire approach to prayer changed. It was as if I had been handed a golden key that unlocked the gates of heaven. From that moment on, I had a personal friend who helped me speak to the Father in Jesus' name. He literally guided me to my knees and made it easy to communicate with the Father.

What a fellowship! That is what the Holy Spirit longs for—your *fellowship!*

Let me explain. There are no requests or petitions in fellowship as there are in prayer. If I asked, "Would you please bring me some food?" That's a request. But fellowship is much more personal. "How are you today? Let's have breakfast together!" That's fellowship.

Remember, there are no selfish requests in fellowship—just friendship, love, and communion. That's how it was with me. I began to wait for the Holy Spirit before I prayed. I would say, "Precious Holy Spirit, would you now come and help me to pray?"

The Bible says, "Likewise the Spirit also helps in our weaknesses. For we do not know what we should pray for as we ought, but the Spirit Himself makes intercession for us with groanings which cannot be uttered. Now He who searches the heart knows what the mind of the Spirit is, because He makes intercession for the saints according to the will of God" (Rom. 8:26–27).

When we don't know what to say He comes to our aid.

And here is the next principle I learned. *The Holy Spirit is the only teacher of the Bible.* "Now we have received, not the spirit of the world, but the Spirit who is from God, that we might know the things that have been freely given to us by God. These things we also speak, not in words which man's wisdom teaches but which the Holy Spirit teaches, comparing spiritual things with spiritual" (1 Cor. 2:12–13).

Accompanied by the Spirit

From my first encounter with the Holy Spirit, I began to know that He was the great teacher—the one who would lead me "into all truth." That is why I asked Him, "Would you please tell me what this Scripture means?"

But I still wanted to know, "Who are You? And why are You so different?" I would say, "I'd like to know what You are like."

Gentle Yet Powerful

Here is what I saw. What He revealed to me was a mighty person and a childlike person at the same time. He said to me, "When you hurt a child he will stay away from you; when you love a child, he will be very close to you." And that is how I began to approach Him. I felt that He was gentle, and yet He is mighty and powerful. Like a child, however, He wants to stay ever so close to those who love Him.

Have you ever seen a little boy or a little girl tugging at Mother's skirt or Father's trousers? Wherever the parents go, the kids hang on and follow them. It's a sure sign that the kids are loved and cared for. That's the way it is with the Holy Spirit. He stays close to those who love Him.

How was it possible that the great evangelist Charles Finney could preach the gospel and people would be "slain under the power," confessing their sins? What was the power that fell when John Wesley stood on the tombstones and opened his mouth to preach? It was the person of the Holy Spirit that *accompanied* their ministry.

In New York City, Kathryn Kuhlman had just finished preaching at a Full Gospel Business Men's convention. She was taken through the kitchen to an elevator to avoid the crowd. The cooks had no idea a meeting was going on and had never heard of Miss Kuhlman. In their white hats and aprons, the cooks didn't even know she was walking by, and the next thing you know they were flat on the floor. Why? Kathryn didn't pray for them; she just walked. What happened? When she left the meeting it seemed as though the power of His presence attended her.

Who is the Holy Spirit? *He is the power of the Lord.*

That power became most evident to me when I began praying in my room—all alone. Day after day, hour after hour, I lifted my hands and said, "Precious Holy Spirit, would You come now and just talk to me?" Where else could I turn? My family was against me. My friends were few. Only Him. Only the Holy Spirit.

There were times when He came in like a wind. Like a fresh breeze on a summer day. The joy of the Lord would fill me until I could contain no more. As we talked I would say, "Holy Spirit, I love You and I long for Your fellowship." And I found out it was mutual. He longed for my fellowship, too.

Supper Can Wait!

Once, in England, I was staying in the home of a Christian family. My room was at the very top of the house. One evening I was lost in the Spirit, having the greatest time in the world talking to Him. The woman of the house called up, "Benny, supper is ready."

But I was bubbling over and didn't want to leave. She called again, "Supper is ready." And as I was about to leave, I felt someone take my hand and say, "Five more minutes. Just five more minutes." The Holy Spirit longed for my fellowship.

You ask, "What did you talk about?" I asked Him questions.

For example, one day I asked, "How can You be distinct from the Father and the Son?" And instantly He showed me Stephen being stoned and He said to me, "Stephen saw the Father and the Son and I was in him." Three distinct individuals.

The Holy Spirit was the one who gave Stephen the power to endure the suffering. Jesus was the one waiting for His coming. And the Father was the one who sat on the throne. You can read about it in Acts 7:54–56.

And the Holy Spirit showed me more.

He was the one who gave Moses the power to be the deliverer of the children of Israel.

He was the power in the life of Joshua.

He was the force behind the wind that divided the Red Sea.

He was the mighty power that smashed the walls of Jericho.

He was the energy behind David's rock when Goliath fell.

The Holy Spirit. He was the force in the life of Samuel, in Elijah—and in Christ the Lord.

Jesus was a total man, yet the Scripture is clear that He would not preach without the Holy Spirit. He would not lay His hands on the sick without the Holy Spirit. "The Spirit of the LORD is upon Me," He said, as He began His ministry, "because He has anointed Me to preach the gospel . . ." (Luke 4:18).

What happened when Jesus returned to the Father? Suddenly the disciples were in such fellowship with the Spirit that their entire vocabulary changed. They began to say that "the Holy Spirit and us" were witnesses of His resurrection. He became a part of every action of their life. They were in total fellowship—working together for the Son.

What was it in the life of the apostle Paul that gave him the power to endure? And what was it in the life of Peter that even his shadow would heal the sick? It was the touch of the Spirit.

David Wilkerson speaks about going to see a woman of God named Mother Basilia Schlink. He said that the moment he entered the room he could feel the presence of the Lord. Why? Because she loved the Holy Spirit. And those who love Him know His presence.

Do You Recognize That Voice?

When Jesus was on the earth and the disciples had a problem, to whom did they turn? They went to the Son and asked, "What should we do?" And He instructed them. But when Christ returned to the Father, they were not left alone. Jesus said to them, "The Holy Spirit will guide you. He will comfort you. He will counsel you and will remind you of things I have told you. He will tell you about Me."

Peter and John were now saying, "Wonderful Holy Spirit." Paul spoke of His "fellowship."

After Peter had his vision on the rooftop of Simon the Tanner's home in Joppa, "the Spirit said to him . . . 'three men are seeking you. Arise therefore, go down and go with them, doubting nothing; for I have sent them'" (Acts 10:19–20).

Peter recognized the voice of the Holy Spirit. And that was the beginning of the gospel being preached to the Gentiles.

How was the Ethiopian eunuch converted? "The Spirit said to Philip, 'Go near and overtake this chariot'" (Acts 8:29). *Philip recognized the voice of the Holy Spirit.* It wasn't God the Father that spoke to him—nor God the Son. It was God the Holy Spirit. He is a person with a will, and that moment He was doing the work of the Father. I believe the greatest sin against the Holy Spirit is grieving Him, which amounts to denying His power and presence. Nowhere in Scripture can you find the words, "Grieve not God the Father" or "Grieve not God the Son." But throughout the Bible you find, "Grieve not the Spirit."

God said to the children of Israel in the wilderness, "You have vexed *My Spirit.*" He didn't say, "You have grieved Me." God the Son looked at the Pharisees and said, "anyone who speaks a word against the Son of Man, it will be forgiven him; but to him who blasphemes against the Holy Spirit, it will not be forgiven" (Luke 12:10).

The person of the Holy Spirit is distinct in the Godhead. He is tender. He is sensitive. But because Jesus gave Him to you and to me, He is not going to leave us.

The Holy Spirit is a gentleman. He doesn't enter your room until you invite Him. He doesn't sit down until you ask Him. And He doesn't speak to you until you speak to Him.

How long will He wait? Until you speak to Him. It could be months—even years. He will just wait and wait and wait. My friend, you will never know His power; you will never know His presence until you go and sit beside Him and say, "Wonderful Holy Spirit, tell me all about Jesus."

I Could Hardly Hold the Phone

After finishing a radio talk show in Florida, the woman who interviewed me said, "Benny, I've been a Christian for a long time, but something is missing in my life."

"What are you hungry for?" I asked.

She said, "I need the reality of God in my life."

I asked her if she knew God the Holy Spirit. "I know Jesus," she said.

"The Holy Spirit is a person," I told her. "How would I feel if you were sitting here ignoring me? When we meet, I expect you to talk with me. And that's the way it is with the Holy Spirit."

"I've never thought of it that way," she said.

"When you are alone tonight, talk to Him," I said. "It's as simple as that." I knew she would find the reality she was seeking.

"What about Jesus?" she asked.

I told her, "Just sit there and wait for Him; He is the one who glorifies Jesus. No, you are not forgetting Jesus. After all, it was Christ that gave you the Holy Spirit. Just do what Jesus said."

The next day I received a phone call from the most excited talk show host you could imagine. "Do you know what happened to me last night?" she asked, talking so fast I had to slow her down. "Benny, the Holy Spirit spoke to me."

What she said made me tingle all over. I could hardly hold the phone. She began to cry as she told me the Holy Spirit said to her, "I have searched the world over and there is no one like Jesus." And she told me of the words she heard: "Come, Lord Jesus. Come, Lord Jesus."

Immediately I was reminded of the words, "The Spirit and the bride say, 'Come'" (Rev. 22:17).

Here is one of the most important lessons I have learned. *A person who knows the presence of the Holy Spirit will always glorify and magnify Jesus.*

When you really know the Spirit, you will glorify Jesus Christ the Son of God because the Holy Spirit within you will glorify God the Son. It's automatic. Only Jesus is glorified in a life that's filled with the Spirit.

Every action of your life reflects what you fill your life with. If you fill your life with newspapers, you will speak news. If you watch soap operas, you will speak soap operas. But if you are filled with the Spirit and you absorb yourself in His presence, you will seek Jesus and glorify no one but Jesus.

If God the Father and God the Son demonstrated their love for the Holy Spirit, how can we do less?

God loved Him so much that He chastised the children of Israel for their disobedience: "But they rebelled and grieved His Holy Spirit; so He turned Himself against them as an enemy" (Isa. 63:10). God would not allow a sacrifice nor even the prayers of Moses to supply forgiveness for sinning against the Holy Spirit.

The High Cost of Lying

The experience of Ananias and Sapphira makes clear what will happen to people who disregard the Spirit. The couple sold a piece of property and only gave a small portion of what belonged to God. Peter said, "Ananias, why has Satan filled your heart to lie to the Holy Spirit?" (Acts 5:3). Ananias died instantly. A few hours later his wife rushed up and Peter asked, "Tell me, is this the price you and Ananias got for the land?"

"Yes," she said, "that is the price." Peter said to her, "'How is it that you have agreed together to test the Spirit of the Lord? Look, the feet of those who have buried your husband are at the door, and they will carry you out.' Then immediately she fell down at his feet and breathed her last" (Acts 5:7–10).

Sin against the Spirit is dangerous. If you don't understand the works of the Spirit, don't talk about them; it is better to keep quiet. In my own services I pray that everything I do will be in His perfect will. The Holy Spirit is the one who called me, and He is the one who controls my meetings. In other words, He's the boss of the service.

You need to ask Him to take charge of your life too.

Why? Because He's the one that was sent to be with you—and in you—forever. You can know Him and have fellowship with Him. And the more you commune with Him, the greater Jesus becomes. And the lovelier Christ becomes. Because everything He talks about is Jesus. Christ said, "When the Helper comes, whom I shall send to you from the Father, the Spirit of truth who proceeds from the Father, He will testify of Me" (John 15:26).

So if I want to know about Jesus, I must go to the Holy Spirit. Jesus said it. And He knew what He was talking about.

In the Old Testament, Moses could go to the Father. In the New Testament, the disciples could talk to the Son. But when you and I have a need, where should we turn? To the Holy Spirit. He is a person, and He is waiting right now for you to welcome Him into your life.

By seeking His presence you will discover the secret of the great men and women of God. David said, "Do not cast me away from Your presence, and do not take Your Holy Spirit from me" (Ps. 51:11). He knew too well what happened when the Spirit left Saul.

Paul told us to walk in the Spirit, live in the Spirit, pray in the Spirit. Peter and Philip spoke to Him. And so did Christ.

It's Time to Begin

You ask, "How do I begin?" It's really very simple. You might start by saying, "Holy Spirit, help me pray now." That's exactly what He wants you to do. The Bible says He prays for you "with groanings that cannot be uttered." And when you begin you will feel your burden being lifted. You'll have a prayer partner who will lead you straight to the throne of God.

The Holy Spirit is such a lovely person. He wants to be your dearest friend, and He is waiting to bring you closer to Jesus. Christ said, "If I do not go away, the Helper will not come to you; but if I depart, I will send Him to you" (John 16:7). Then He said the Holy Spirit "will guide you into all truth" and will "glorify Me, for He will take of what is Mine and declare it to you" (John 16:13–14). And not only that—He'll prepare you for the coming of the Lord so that when the Rapture takes place, you'll be ready.

The Holy Spirit is waiting. He wants you to begin a new relationship—person to person.

FIVE

Whose Voice Do You Hear?

"Benny, I want you to stop talking about Jesus in this house. Do you understand?" I can never forget the angry voice of my father, who was infuriated by my conversion. And after my encounter with the Holy Spirit, his wrath grew even worse.

But I began to hear another voice. It was the sound of the Spirit, and He gave me a love for my father that surpassed anything I had known as a child or as a teen. No matter what my father said, I could just look at him with total peace. And it seemed that the more angry he became, the more love the Spirit gave me.

Three things happened when the Holy Spirit entered my life.

First, the Word of the Living God became absolute life to me. No longer did I read a little from Matthew and a little from the Psalms. I opened the Bible and felt as if I were inside of it—seeing it "live and in living color." The voice of the Holy Spirit led me to a great adventure in the Scriptures.

Second, my prayer life changed completely. Gone were the

hours of praying, yawning, and repeating myself. The Holy Spirit and I were in conversation. He made God real. He gave me power and a boldness that made me feel ten feet tall.

And third, He transformed my daily Christian life. I actually began to sing and didn't know why until I read the words: "Be filled with the Spirit, speaking to one another in psalms and hymns and spiritual songs, singing and making melody in your heart to the Lord" (Eph. 5:18-19).

What began to happen to me was not natural—it was *supernatural*. The Spirit had taken over. He began to baptize me with a love for people—and especially for my own father. It was exactly as the Word declared: "The love of God has been poured out in our hearts by the Holy Spirit who was given to us" (Rom. 5:5).

I became such a changed person that my natural instincts and reactions were replaced by the leading of the Spirit. I learned what it meant to "crucify the flesh." And I realized that I couldn't do it by myself. "For if you live according to the flesh you will die; but if by the Spirit you put to death the deeds of the body, you will live. For as many as are led by the Spirit of God, these are sons of God" (Rom. 8:13-14).

His Voice

How are you led by the Spirit? *You become familiar with His voice.* You recognize it. You respond to it. And the more you fellowship with Him, the deeper the relationship becomes.

In the Beginning

From the beginning of time, God made the person and the power of the Holy Spirit clear. In fact, the Holy Spirit is the first manifestation of the Godhead in Scripture. "And the Spirit of God was hovering over the face of the waters" (Gen. 1:2).

When God created Adam out of the dust of the ground He began by forming mud. That mud was absolutely dead until the breath of life came. The Bible says that God "breathed into his nostrils the breath of life; and man became a living being" (Gen. 2:7).

The breath of God is the Holy Ghost. Here is how Job described it: "The Spirit of God has made me, and the breath of the Almighty gives me life" (Job 33:4).

The moment God breathed into Adam, he came alive. When Adam opened his eyes the first contact he had was with the Holy Ghost. For He was the breath that flowed through Adam's body and remained hovering over him. Adam stood up completely filled with the presence of God.

The Scripture tells me that God the Holy Spirit was the power of creation. "By His Spirit He adorned the heavens" (Job 26:13).

What is even more exciting, however, is that God wants to take that same Spirit and give Him to you. He actually wants to "pour" Him on you:

> Until the Spirit is poured upon us from on high,
> And the wilderness becomes a fruitful field,
> And the fruitful field is counted as a forest.
> Then justice will dwell in the wilderness,
> And righteousness remain in the fruitful
>   field. (Isa. 32:15–16)

What a wonderful promise. God wants to pour His Spirit on you. He wants to breathe His Spirit into you. He wants you, like Adam, to come alive!

Realizing that the breath of God is the Spirit of God was for me like discovering a buried treasure. Have you ever heard the voice of the Almighty speaking to you? Many people have. But exactly who was speaking? Whose voice did you hear?

I believe you hear the Holy Spirit. He is the one who communicates the voice of God. The description of God the Father's voice is recorded in Job,

> Hear attentively the thunder of His voice. . . .
> He thunders with His majestic voice. . . .
> God thunders marvelously with His voice;
> He does great things which we cannot
> comprehend. (Job 37:2, 4–5)

The power of God's voice was more than the people of Israel could understand.

A Voice from Heaven

How did God speak to Moses? Through an angel.

In the New Testament, there were only three times that God actually spoke. First, He spoke of Jesus: "And suddenly a voice came from heaven, saying, 'This is My beloved Son, in whom I am well pleased'" (Matt. 3:17).

Then Jesus Himself asked the Father to "glorify Your name." And here is what happened: "Then a voice came from heaven, saying, 'I have both glorified it and will glorify it again'" (John 12:28). The crowd who heard it said it had "thundered" (v. 29).

The only other time God directly spoke was when the clouds surrounded the disciples on the Mount of Transfiguration and He said, "This is My beloved Son, in whom I am well pleased. Hear Him" (Matt. 17:5). Again, the voice of God produced an awesome result. "When the disciples heard this, they fell on their faces and were greatly afraid. But Jesus came and touched them and said, 'Arise, and do not be afraid.' When they had lifted up their eyes, they saw no one but Jesus only" (vv. 6–8).

You say, "Benny, I thought God spoke throughout the Word." Exactly right. But the one who was speaking was the Holy Ghost.

Let me give you an example. The voice that was heard by the prophets was that of the Spirit—not the voice of the Son or of the Father.

Isaiah talks about hearing the voice of the Lord saying

> Go, and tell this people:
> "Keep on hearing, but do not understand;
> Keep on seeing, but do not perceive."
> Make the heart of this people dull,
> And their ears heavy,
> And shut their eyes;
> Lest they see with their eyes,
> And hear with their ears,
> And understand with their heart,
> And return and be healed. (Isa. 6:9–10)

But who was really speaking? Was it really the voice of the Lord? Or was it the voice of Jehovah on earth—the Holy Spirit? To find out, let's look at that same Scripture as it was repeated in the book of Acts.

Paul, in Rome under the watchful eye of a guard, preached that

> The Holy Spirit spoke rightly through Isaiah the
>   prophet to our fathers, saying,
> "Go to this people and say: 'Hearing you will hear,
>   and shall not understand;

And seeing you will see, and not perceive;

For the heart of this people has grown dull.

Their ears are hard of hearing,

And their eyes they have closed,

Lest they should see with their eyes and hear with their ears,

Lest they should understand with their hearts and turn,

So that I should heal them.'" (Acts 28:25–27)

Who really spoke those words? What Isaiah attributed to the Lord, Paul clarified as being spoken by the Holy Spirit.

Remember that the New Testament explains the Old. Here's another example. In Jeremiah we read: "But this is the covenant that I will make with the house of Israel after those days, says the LORD: I will put My law in their minds, and write it on their hearts; and I will be their God, and they shall be My people" (Jer. 31:33).

The prophet writes, "says the LORD," but to understand the true source of that Scripture, you need to read it in the book of Hebrews: "The Holy Spirit also witnesses to us; for after He had said before, 'This is the covenant that I will make with them after those days, says the Lord: I will put My laws into their hearts, and in their minds I will write them'" (Heb. 10: 15–16).

Who said it? *The Holy Spirit.* Not only did He witness it, but Scripture reveals that "He had said before" (v. 15).

Who Is "Jehovah"?

A profound change took place in my spiritual life when I realized that the Holy Ghost was God. Millions of people—and I was among them—are somehow brought up to believe that He is less equal. We are somehow indoctrinated that because He comes third He is not really God.

You must come to this truth: *The Holy Spirit is God.* He is no less

God than Jesus. He is no less God than the Father. He's as much God as the Father and the Son.

Jehovah is the name of the triune being—not the name of just one of them. The Father is called Jehovah. The Son is called Jehovah. The Holy Ghost is called Jehovah.

When God the Father speaks, He speaks through the voice of the Holy Spirit. When Jesus sent out the Twelve, He said, "Do not worry about how or what you should speak. For it will be given to you in that hour what you should speak; for it is not you who speak, but the Spirit of your Father who speaks in you" (Matt. 10:19–20).

Over and over again in Revelation we are advised, "He who has an ear, let him hear what the Spirit says . . ." (Rev. 2:7, 11, 17). Whose voice should we hear? The voice of the Spirit.

Even Christ Himself does not speak without the Holy Ghost. In Acts we read that He was taken up into heaven, ". . . after He through the Holy Spirit had given commandments to the apostles whom He had chosen" (Acts 1:2). And in Hebrews we find that Christ offered Himself to God "through the eternal Spirit" (Heb. 9:14).

Is it becoming clear? *The Holy Spirit is the one who communicates heaven into your heart.* He is the voice of God to you. You say, "Well, I know it was God speaking to me." Of course it was God. It was God the Holy Spirit. To put it another way, it is the Father, through the Son, speaking by the Spirit.

From what you have already learned, you can imagine what would happen if God the Father ever spoke to you audibly. You could not bear it. I doubt that you are even prepared to hear the voice of Jesus, described as "the sound of many waters" (Rev. 1:15). When John heard it, he fell at His feet "as dead" (v.17).

The Holy Spirit, however, takes the voice of the Father and the Son and makes it quiet, lovely, and perfectly clear.

The moment that I realized that the Holy Spirit was God—and

began to worship Him and treat Him as God—my life began to change. No longer did I see the Holy Ghost as some lesser, weaker, mist-shrouded being standing in a corner. No longer were God the Father and God the Son receiving all of my worship.

Let me say it again. *The Holy Spirit is God*—equal in majesty, power, glory, and eternity. He's God.

What did Jesus say about the Spirit? He said that when He comes, "He will not speak on His own authority, but whatever He hears He will speak" (John 16:13). What does He hear? The precious Holy Spirit hears the Father and speaks directly to you. But when He speaks, He doesn't say, "The Father says." He says, "I say." Why? Because Father, Son, and Holy Spirit always act in harmony.

Like the Sun in the Sky

It is so easy to limit the Godhead or to divide the Godhead unscripturally. Young Christians often ask, "How can God be one and three at the same time?" God is one. But God is three: Father, Son, and Holy Ghost. And while this book dwells on the Holy Spirit, I am distinguishing them on purpose to show you the tri-une being.

God is like the sun in the sky. If you look at its brightness you see one sun. In reality, however, it is a triune sun that keeps our planet alive. There are three distinct elements: the sun, light, and heat.

And so it is with the Trinity. The Father is like the whole sun, Jesus is the light, and the Holy Ghost is the heat you feel. When you stand in the presence of the Father, what do you feel? The warmth, the energy, and power of the Holy Spirit. If you look into the face of the Father, whom do you see? "He who has seen Me has seen the Father," Jesus said to Philip (John 14:9).

I get excited when I think about the time I enter heaven. The

Godhead will be there. When I stand before the Father I will see all three—the Spirit, the Son, and God Himself.

What does God look like? There's not one place in the Word of God where the Father is described in detail. Stephen, "being full of the Holy Spirit, gazed into heaven and saw the glory of God, and Jesus standing at the right hand of God" (Acts 7:55).

Stephen saw Jesus clearly, but when he saw the Father he could only see the "glory" that surrounded Him. Yes, God the Father has a form but no man knows what it looks like (Phil. 2:6). The Word says, "No one has seen God at any time" (John 1:18), but the Son came to reveal Him.

If you look closely at what Christ said, you will understand how the Spirit embraces the Godhead. Jesus said, "No one comes to the Father except through Me" (John 14:6). And Scripture teaches that we are drawn to Christ by the Spirit. In other words, *you've got to have the Spirit if you want the Godhead.* When you embrace the Holy Ghost, you are also embracing the Father and the Son.

I will never forget the day that the Holy Spirit revealed to me that His Lordship is equal to that of Jesus. He showed me in Scripture that He is called *Lord.*

Paul, writing to the church at Corinth, says, "Now the Lord is the Spirit; and where the Spirit of the Lord is, there is liberty" (2 Cor. 3:17). That's right. We all confess that Jesus is Lord—but so is the Holy Spirit. *He is the Spirit of Jesus!*

The Holy Spirit is omnipresent, but unfortunately liberty and freedom are not found everywhere. Some churches feel more like a hostile prison than a house of praise. Why? Because the Spirit is not Lord in that congregation.

Never forget it: *The Lord is the Spirit!* In the very next verse Paul writes, "But we all, with unveiled face, beholding as in a mirror the glory of the Lord, are being transformed into the same image from glory to glory, just as by the Spirit of the Lord" (v. 18).

How Do You Know?

Next, you need to understand that the Trinity is the glory of God. God the Father is the glory of God; God the Son is the glory of God; and God the Holy Spirit is the glory of God. But who manifests that glory? It is the Holy Spirit. That is part of His work.

Let me ask another question. Do you know that you have been saved from your sin? Well, how do you know it? Did you hear a celestial voice from heaven? Did Jesus appear in a physical body and say, "You are saved"?

How do you know that you have passed from spiritual death unto life? You know it because the Spirit told you. You know it so strongly you'll die for it. Why? Because when the Holy Ghost speaks, He speaks right into your being—into your very blood and marrow.

In exactly the same way, we know that Jesus is alive. Not because we have seen His face, but we know He is alive by His Spirit. And that same Spirit is the third person of the Trinity.

Someone recently asked me, "Benny, how do you know you are saved?" All I could say was, "I know that I know, that I know, that I know, that I know." That's the strength, the assurance, the Holy Spirit has given to me.

The Spirit is not only the voice you hear; He is also the mighty power that you feel. The prophet Micah said, "But truly I am full of power by the Spirit of the LORD, and of justice and might" (Mic. 3:8). *The Holy Spirit is the might of the Godhead.* Even the angel said to Mary as she was about to give birth to Jesus, "The Holy Spirit will come upon you, and the power of the Highest will overshadow you" (Luke 1:35). He is that pre-eminent power.

The Holy Spirit is also your great defender. For example: Who do you think protects you from the attacks of Satan? It is the Holy Spirit. "When the enemy comes in like a flood, the Spirit of the LORD will lift up a standard against him" (Isa. 59:19). When you read that familiar verse you come to the conclusion that the enemy comes in like a flood. But I've got news for you: the flood is the Holy Ghost, not the devil. You see, in the Hebrew there are no commas. But the King James translator put a comma after the word *flood,* and made the enemy more powerful than he actually is. The actual Hebrew says that when the enemy comes in "like a flood the spirit comes against him."

"Follow Me!"

Who keeps you safe? The Holy Spirit. That is the task assigned to Him by Christ. So often we call Him Jesus, but He is actually the Spirit of Jesus. Again, we only separate them for discussion's sake so we can better understand them because they are really one in Being. Because *where the Holy Ghost is, Jesus is—and the Father is.* When the Holy Ghost talks to you, all three are talking, but the Holy Ghost is the one you hear. The Holy Ghost is the one you sense. The Holy Ghost is the one leading you in the will of the Father.

When I first read the words of Jesus, "Follow me," I wondered how that would be possible. Were his followers expected to rise with Him at the Ascension? Of course not. When Christ returned to the Father He sent the Holy Spirit, saying, "He will guide you" (John 16:13). Jesus was saying, "Stop following me. I'm leaving, but I'm now sending the Holy Spirit. You must now follow Him." So why do we say, "I'm following Jesus!" when the only guide we have is the Holy Spirit?

Following His Voice

From the moment of my first encounter with the Spirit I knew I must follow His voice. There were only two options. Either I could follow the sound of a carnal, fleshly world, or I could follow Him: "Those who live according to the flesh set their minds on the things of the flesh, but those who live according to the Spirit, the things of the Spirit" (Rom. 8:5).

It's as basic as life itself. If you desire the flesh, you will follow the flesh; but if your heart yearns for the Spirit, you'll be drawn to Him like a magnet. It starts with desire. For me, I had one great question; "How can I really know You?" That question was the cry of my heart. My great hunger was to know the Holy Spirit personally. I was not disappointed.

Paul tells you to "walk in the Spirit, and you shall not fulfill the lust of the flesh. For the flesh lusts against the Spirit, and the Spirit against the flesh; and these are contrary to one another, so that you do not do the things that you wish. But if you are led by the Spirit, you are not under the law" (Gal. 5:16–18).

An amazing thing happened to the apostle Paul and his companions during their missionary travels. They went to Phrygia and Galatia, having been "forbidden by the Holy Spirit to preach the word in Asia. After they had come to Mysia, they tried to go into Bithynia, but the Spirit did not permit them" (Acts 16:6–7). That's right. They were so in tune with the voice of the Spirit they probably said, "Well, if He's not going, we're not going either."

But perhaps the most revealing words in the account were that they were kept "by the Holy Spirit." When Christ returned to the Father, the Holy Spirit began to do the work of Christ on earth.

Have you begun to recognize His voice? Paul did. During that same journey the Spirit, through a vision, showed the apostle a man from a far country standing and begging him, "Come over to Macedonia and help us" (v. 9). Paul left at once.

Your Conscience Confirms It

How does the Holy Spirit speak? He witnesses to your very conscience. In Paul's letter to the church at Rome, he says, "I tell the truth in Christ, I am not lying, my conscience also bearing me witness in the Holy Spirit" (Rom. 9:1).

You should never doubt the leading of the Holy Spirit. At a time when your "inner man" is troubled, don't move. If you attempt to be your own guide, you'll literally collapse. Listen to His voice as He speaks to your very soul.

During a church building program I was asked, "How do you know you're doing the right thing?" The answer was the same as if I'd been asked about my salvation. "I know that I know, that I know, that I know." The Lord, through the Holy Spirit, told me to start building. Every decision in my life is based on that same inner voice.

The worldly don't have the foggiest notion of the things of the Spirit. That's because they are spiritually blind. But *you* can know. Why? Because you understand how the Spirit operates and you are learning to recognize His voice.

It's the same way we know that heaven is real though we have never entered the pearly gates. It has been made alive to us by the Spirit. Reading about heaven in the Word is wonderful, but that is not what gives you the reality. Countless millions have read the Bible and are still bound for eternal damnation. Why? The Word did not enter their hearts.

Here's the answer. He has given you the understanding of a new covenant "not of the letter but of the Spirit; for the letter kills, but the Spirit gives life" (2 Cor. 3:6).

73

It is amazing to me how someone can read Scripture and say, "No. I don't think He meant that." Or, "He didn't really perform that miracle." Or, "He wasn't born of the Virgin Mary." The problem is simple; they are thinking with a carnal mind.

But you can discuss the same issues with absolute assurance. It was not what you read; it was what the Holy Spirit told you. And you'd stake your life on it!

If you truly want to understand how the Holy Spirit speaks, read and reread these profound words: "The Spirit Himself bears witness with our spirit that we are children of God" (Rom. 8:16). How do we know it is true? *His* spirit bears witness with *our* spirit. Again, you *know that you know.*

The Holy Spirit is God the witness. What did Peter say when the apostles were called before the Sanhedrin? "We are His witnesses to these things, and so also is the Holy Spirit whom God has given to those who obey Him" (Acts 5:32). It is that continuing confirmation that keeps you in the center of God's will.

If there was one particular verse the Holy Spirit revealed to me that turned my life around, it was this: "The grace of the Lord Jesus Christ, and the love of God, and the communion of the Holy Spirit *be* with you all. Amen" (2 Cor. 13:14).

The Spirit brought this verse before me again and again. And the more I studied it, the more excited I became. Suddenly I knew that the Holy Spirit was for me—today.

Here's what the Holy Spirit showed me. When did we know "the grace of the Lord Jesus Christ"? When He died for us. When did we know "the love of God"? When we saw the cross. They both refer to the past. But then we read, "the communion of the Holy Ghost, *be* with you all." I said, "That's it. The Holy Spirit is here to commune with me and to *be* with me, now!"

What a Communion!

What does the Scripture mean when it talks about "communion"? There are seven meanings.

First, the word communion means *presence*. God the Father's desire for you is that the sweet presence of the Holy Spirit will be with you.

Second, it means *fellowship*. You do not need to pray to the Holy Spirit; you simply fellowship with Him. And you should seek that communion as you would seek water in the wilderness.

The third meaning is *sharing together*. You pour out your heart and He pours out His. You share your joy and He shares His. "It seemed good to the Holy Spirit, and to us . . ." wrote the apostles to the believers in Antioch (Acts 15:28). They were sharing—even writing letters—together.

Fourth, communion means *participation with*. The Holy Spirit becomes your partner. The Scripture, filled with phrases like "working with them" and "the Spirit and us," makes it clear that the work of the Spirit is in participation with you.

Fifth, it means *intimacy*. You'll never experience a deep love with Christ until you know it with the Holy Spirit who brings that intimacy. There is no other way. God has "poured out" His love into our hearts "by the Holy Spirit who was given to us" (Rom. 5:5). You can't love God without the Holy Ghost.

Sixth, the word means *friendship*. The Spirit longs to be your closest friend, someone with whom you can share the deepest secrets of your heart.

And seventh, communion means *comradeship*. In Greek the word means "commander." He's like a captain, a ruler, or a boss—but a loving, friendly one. Just as He instructed the apostles where they should go and where they shouldn't, He must be allowed to rule in your personal affairs. Remember, since Christ departed, The Holy Spirit is "in charge" on earth.

Are you listening for His voice? Are you ready to commune with Him?

When I began my fellowship with the Holy Spirit I talked with Him day and night. Not a day passed that I did not say, "Holy Spirit. Precious Holy Spirit." And we began our time of prayer and communication.

Oh, the sound of His voice.

SIX

Spirit, Soul, and Body

Satan, the great deceiver, has done an incredible job.

He has convinced the world—even dedicated ministers of the gospel—that the Holy Spirit is nothing more than an influence or a special power. This deception is a priority of Satan because he knows that the moment you discover the personality and reality of the Spirit, your life will be dramatically transformed.

Just look at history. Every great revival was accompanied by a revelation of the Holy Spirit. Even Martin Luther credits the great Reformation to the work of the Spirit. He said that Galatians was his favorite book in Scripture because of the verse that says, "Walk in the Spirit, and you shall not fulfill the lust of the flesh" (Gal. 5:16).

But today few people know what it means to "walk" in the Spirit. The root of the word means in unison with, one with, or connected to—even fellowship with. It's astounding, but people who have been raised in a "spirit-filled" church have asked me: "Am I supposed to talk to the Spirit?"

Recently I was invited to speak in a large historic Pentecostal church, and the congregation was shocked when I said, "You are the ones who have rediscovered the Holy Spirit, but you have placed Him in a cage." I explained, "You thought that the Catholics couldn't have Him. You thought that the Baptists couldn't have Him. But I've got news for you. He's jumped over your fence and walked into Saint Michael's, First Baptist, United Methodist, and all the rest."

Millions of people have been touched by the Spirit, but their spiritual growth has been stunted by clergy who, for whatever reasons, choose to subordinate the third person of the Trinity.

Unfortunately the Church of Jesus Christ has ignored what I am sharing with you. The fact that you are reading this book, however, tells me that you have a personal hunger to know the Holy Spirit. You can be "filled" with the Spirit and have an undeniable encounter with Him, but a deep understanding of the Holy Ghost does not come overnight. For me it has taken years and years of His leading and revelation in Scripture. And I am still learning every day.

The Godhead

What I am about to share with you regarding the Godhead gave me an entirely new picture of the Father, the Son, and the Holy Spirit. I found that God is eternal spirit yet with nonmaterial form, but He often reveals Himself through human form and other human traits.

God the Father

What about the way God frequently appears to man? When Ezekiel had his vision of God in 593 B.C., he described Him seated above an expanse that separated creatures from the glory of the Lord. He saw "the likeness of a throne, in appearance like a sapphire stone, . . . with the appearance of a man high above it" (Ezek. 1:26). What was the appearance of God the Father? Like that of a man.

You say, "I've been taught that God is spirit." Yes, but He is spirit with mysterious form, not some cloud floating in space. The apostle John, in Revelation, described Him as the reflected brilliance of precious stones. He said, "Immediately I was in the Spirit, and behold, a throne set in heaven, and One sat on the throne. And He who sat there was like a jasper and a sardius stone in appearance" (Rev. 4:2–3).

The prophets describe the features of God in great detail. Isaiah says, "His lips are full of indignation, and His tongue like a devouring fire. His breath is like an overflowing stream" (Isa. 30:27–28).

And God revealed the fact that He can see. "They did evil before My eyes" (Isa. 66:4).

To my amazement I found that God is described as having the likeness of fingers and hands and a face. After the Lord spoke to Moses on Mount Sinai, He gave him the tablets of stone, "written with the finger of God" (Ex. 31:18). Then the Lord said to Moses, "You cannot see My face, for no man shall see Me, and live" (Ex. 33:20).

He even talked to Moses about His "back." He said, "While My glory passes by . . . I . . . will cover you with My hand while I pass by. Then I will take away My hand, and you shall see My back; but My face shall not be seen" (vv. 22–23).

If God reveals Himself as only invisible spirit, how was it possible that Adam and Eve heard His footsteps? "And they heard the sound of the LORD God walking in the garden in the cool of the day" (Gen. 3:8).

God also has a heart: "The LORD was sorry that He had made man on the earth, and He was grieved in His heart" (Gen. 6:6).

Like a "Blazing Fire"

Now let's look at the Son.

Before the Lord Jesus came to earth, He, with God the Father, had only an immaterial form. His earthly body of flesh, blood, and bone was given Him when He was born a babe in Bethlehem. And, like you, He grew to be a man.

If I were to ask, "Of the Father, Son, and Holy Ghost, which is a real person?"—most people would say the Son. We can identify with Christ because He took the form of a human being. In fact, if you do not believe that Christ lived, died, and rose from the dead, it is impossible for you to be a Christian. It is the foundation that makes possible your salvation.

The Bible makes it clear that Jesus—part of the Godhead—has a soul. At Gethsemane, before the crucifixion, He said to His disciples, "My soul is exceedingly sorrowful, even to death" (Mark 14:34).

We have a physical description of Christ that shapes our image of Him. We know, for example, that He wore a beard and had long hair. In Old Testament prophecy concerning the suffering of the Messiah, the Lord says, "I gave My back to those who struck Me, And My cheeks to those who plucked out the beard" (Isa. 50:6). Christ was also a Nazarite, from a city where the men customarily wore long hair.

Today, Christ in His resurrected body sits at the right hand of God the Father. And what does He look like? John, in Revelation, saw a vision of Him "clothed with a garment down to the feet and girded about the chest with a golden band. His head and hair were white like wool, as white as snow, and His eyes like a flame of fire. . . . His countenance was like the sun shining in its strength" (Rev. 1:13–14, 16). On His head was "a golden crown" (Rev. 14:14). And on His robe were written the words, "KING OF KINGS AND LORD OF LORDS" (Rev. 19:16).

It is not God the Father that John is talking about. It is the "Son of man." And His glorified human body is distinct from the divine form of God the Father.

A Mind of His Own

But what about the Holy Spirit? Does He also have a mind, a will, and emotions? Does He have a body? He certainly does. It's a subject that most ministers are afraid to discuss, but I have experienced the person of the Holy Ghost.

Without question we all agree He is a "Spirit." That's part of His name. But what about His inner being? Is He really a "person"?

First, the Holy Spirit has a mind of His own. Speaking of the Holy Ghost, Paul said, "Now He who searches the hearts knows what the mind of the Spirit is, because He makes intercession for the saints according to the will of God" (Rom. 8:27). The mind of the Spirit is distinct from that of the Father and the Son.

He also has emotions. He has deep feelings that allow Him to grieve and to love: "And do not grieve the Holy Spirit of God, by whom you were sealed for the day of redemption" (Eph. 4:30). His heart can be touched, and it has the capacity to express love. Paul, writing to the Christians at Rome, said: "I beg you, brethren, through the Lord Jesus Christ, and through the love of the Spirit, that you strive together with me in prayers to God for me" (Rom. 15:30). Can you imagine loving without emotion?

The Person of the Spirit

What about the *will* of the Holy Spirit? Perhaps you have never considered it possible for the Holy Spirit to make His own decisions. He certainly can, but His decisions are always in harmony with the Father's and the Son's. Speaking of spiritual gifts, Paul wrote, "One and the same Spirit works all these things, distributing to each one individually as He wills" (1 Cor. 12:11). In other words, the Holy Spirit makes the decision.

Doves and Lambs

It is the question of the "body" of the Holy Spirit that causes much confusion. A man recently said to me, "Benny, the body of the Holy Spirit is really that of a dove. That's how He descended from Heaven." I replied, "If that's true, then you must believe that Jesus was really a little lamb. That's how He is presented in Revelation."

In the book of the Revelation John the apostle heard an elder say, "Do not weep. Behold, the Lion of the tribe of Judah . . . has prevailed" (Rev. 5:5). He turned, expecting to see a roaring lion, and instead he saw a gentle lamb that had been slain. Now Jesus went to heaven with a physical body, with nailprints in His hands. But the symbol John saw was a lamb. Why? The lamb symbolized the Lamb of God—Jesus Christ.

The Holy Spirit was seen by Jesus immediately following His baptism: "The heavens were opened to Him, and He saw the Spirit of God descending like a dove and alighting upon Him" (Matt. 3:16). Just as the Father and the Son can be seen, so can the Holy Spirit. But His descent as a beautiful dove does not mean that He flies around in heaven like a dove. Nor does Jesus walk around heaven with the body of a lamb.

In Revelation the Holy Ghost was seen again as "seven lamps" of blazing fire (Rev. 4:5). If the Spirit came as a dove in Matthew, you can't expect Him to have a body made out of seven candles or seven pieces of fire. The Holy Ghost is not seven lamps, nor is He a dove. A lamb, a dove, a lamp—*these are all symbols*, not physical forms of bodies.

Hearing, Speaking, Seeing

Scripture, however, tells me that the Holy Spirit can communicate although He doesn't have ears or a mouth. He certainly can

listen and speak to us: "Whatever He hears He will speak" (John 16:13). And we must listen to Him: "Let him hear what the Spirit says" (Rev. 2:7). And even though He doesn't have eyes like mine, "the Spirit searches all things, yes, the deep things of God" (1 Cor. 2:10). Since you were created with ears, a mouth, and eyes, wouldn't you expect the Creator—Father, Son, and Holy Ghost—to be able to understand and talk to you?

I also believe the Holy Ghost can make His presence known through bodily forms, and yet remain without limitation and fully omnipresent. The Bible makes this clear when it says, "The Spirit of God was hovering over the face of the waters" (Gen. 1:2).

Now the Bible does not tell me what He "looks" like. I am told a little of how the Father reveals Himself. And I am given some description of Christ. But details regarding the way the Holy Spirit unveils Himself to us are rare in Scripture. Sometimes He is seen but not heard; other times heard but not seen. At any time, however, He can reveal His presence and message through any kind of form He chooses.

A Striking Resemblance

"What does God the Father sometimes look like?" Although I've never seen Him make a visible, physical appearance, I believe—as with the Holy Spirit—that He can make Himself look like Jesus looked on earth. In fact, many divine character traits are best made known through human nature, which is created in God's image (Gen. 1:26–27; James 3:9).

Hebrews speaks of Christ as "being the brightness of His glory and the express image of His person" (Heb. 1:3). I can only come to one conclusion: When we see Jesus, we see the Father also. And I believe that Jesus reveals the Holy Ghost as He does the Father. Look at Jesus and you see the Spirit too.

Someday soon I'm going to find out for certain. And I believe that you are planning to be there too.

Again, the Holy Spirit is not a heavenly breeze or a hazy cloud floating in and out of your life. He is God, and He resides in us—equal with the Father and the Son in the Trinity. Paul, writing to the church at Corinth, said, "Do you not know that you are the temple of God and that the Spirit of God dwells in you? If anyone defiles the temple of God, God will destroy him. For the temple of God is holy, which temple you are" (1 Cor. 3:16–17). He is saying that the Spirit lives in God's temple. We are that temple, and the Father and the Spirit are equal in us.

Coequal with Father and Son

The Holy Spirit is not simply a person, distinct from the Father and distinct from the Son. He is much more. He's God, coequal with the Father and Christ.

First, we find that *the Holy Ghost is omnipresent*. In other words, He can be at all places at the same time. "Spirits" are not omnipresent, but the Holy Ghost is. He's just as real in Los Angeles as He is in Leningrad. Just as alive. Just as full of glory.

Now some people have needless problems with Satan. They think the devil is omnipresent. Let me assure you that he is not. Satan cannot be at all places at the same time. Why? Because angels cannot be at all places at the same time, and the devil was an angel, an archangel. The angels Michael or Gabriel are not omnipresent, and neither is Satan.

The omnipresence of the Holy Ghost is described in the Psalms:

> Where can I go from Your Spirit?
> Or where can I flee from Your presence?
> If I ascend into heaven, You are there;

If I make my bed in hell, behold, You are there.
If I take the wings of the morning,
And dwell in the uttermost parts of the sea,
Even there Your hand shall lead me,
And Your right hand shall hold me. (Ps. 139: 7–10)

But not only is He omnipresent; *the Holy Spirit is omnipotent—* all powerful. The angel said to Mary, "The Holy Spirit will come upon you, and the power of the Highest will overshadow you" (Luke 1:35). The power of the "Highest" speaks of the Spirit of God. That same power of the Highest is the Holy Ghost, and He is omnipotent. All glorious. All powerful. Almighty God!

The Holy Spirit is also omniscient. He's all knowing. I get excited when I read the words,

> *"Eye has not seen, nor ear heard,*
> *Nor have entered into the heart of man*
> *The things which God has prepared for those who love Him."*

But God has revealed them to us through His Spirit. For the Spirit searches all things, yes, the deep things of God. For what man knows the things of a man except the spirit of the man which is in him? Even so no one knows the things of God except the Spirit of God. (1 Cor. 2:9–11)

Think about it! The Holy Ghost actually searches the mind of God. He finds what's there and presents it to you. He says, "Here's what I've found." How can He search the "deep things of God"? Because He is all knowing.

There's something else you need to know about Satan. He cannot read your mind. Angels can't read your mind, and the devil is an angel. If he could read your mind, he would be an all-knowing spirit. But that place is reserved for the Father and the Holy Ghost. Satan cannot read your mind.

Should He Be Worshiped?

Here is an important question I must ask. If the Holy Spirit is omnipresent, if He is omnipotent, if He is omniscient, should we worship Him as God? Does He deserve our praise and adoration?

Christians have a major problem when it comes to the topic of worshiping the Spirit. It's a subject they would rather not discuss. And if you ask them, "Why don't you worship the Holy Ghost?" they can't seem to find an answer. Oh, they'll say something like, "Well, we're not supposed to."

To be honest, I had the same problem. Why? Because the devil deceived me as he has deluded so many. I thought, "How can I worship Him? It's just not the way I've been taught."

The Holy Ghost, however, is much more than a bird flying in the sky who gives you the pentecostal experience. If He is all the things we've been discussing—equal with the Father and the Son, then He is to be worshiped. After all, don't we worship the Father? And don't we worship the Son?

You may wonder, "How should the Holy Spirit be worshiped?" Well, how do you worship God the Father? And how do you worship the Son? There should be no difference. You should shower Him with your devotion and your love.

The Bible tells us that the Godhead—Father, Son, and Spirit—is self-existent: "How much more shall the blood of Christ, who through the eternal Spirit offered Himself without spot to God, purge your conscience from dead works to serve the living God?" (Heb. 9:14).

When we learn about angels, we find that they only are present because of the existence of Jesus. But I've got news for you. God the Holy Spirit can be referred to as the "I Am," just like God the Father and God the Son.

Oil, Water, Clouds, and Light

Since my first encounter with the Holy Spirit, I have experienced a growing reality of His presence. Every Scripture, every encounter, and every revelation makes my walk in the Spirit more complete.

Recently, during a time of study in the Word, I said to my wife, "You know, I feel the presence of God all over me." Here's what touched me that night while I was tracing the meanings of words and their connection with the Spirit.

I was wondering, "What does it really mean to "grieve" the Spirit?

What I learned was that the Holy Ghost is not just a spirit who can have shape. *He's so real He can be resisted.* Now many people think the Holy Ghost is a wind. But He isn't. That's just another in a long list of descriptive symbols used to communicate the Spirit—oil, water, a dove, a cloud, light, and so many more. It certainly doesn't mean that He looks like His symbols.

Wind is invisible to the eye, but you cannot resist it. The word *resist* means to oppose. You cannot oppose wind. Try to stand against wind and it will pass right by you. Yet you can oppose the Holy Ghost. You can actually stop Him from working. Stephen, in his speech to the Sanhedrin, quoted Moses saying: "You stiff-necked and uncircumcised in heart and ears! You always resist the Holy Spirit; As your fathers did, so do you" (Acts 7:51).

They opposed Him and, unfortunately, they were successful. Remember this: you cannot resist wind, oil, or even a dove that will just fly away, but you *can resist a person*—and that is what the Holy Spirit is.

Then I traced the words *grief* and *grieved* in the original Greek.

The root word is *loopa*. And here is what it means: to feel pain in body and mind. It means to suffer mental and physical anguish.

The Holy Ghost is a person, or Paul would not have said, "Do not grieve the Holy Spirit" (Eph. 4:30). The Holy Ghost doesn't just hurt. Hurt operates at the level of the emotions. He *grieves*, and that goes much deeper.

Not only that, but the Holy Spirit can be *quenched*. The word means to put out. Paul warned the church at Thessalonica, "Do not quench the Spirit" (1 Thess. 5:19). You cannot quench the wind or other symbols. But you can stop a person. And that is what the Holy Spirit is.

So Easily Wounded

You also need to realize that the Holy Spirit can be afflicted and tormented. He can be *vexed*. Isaiah talked about the lovingkindness of the Lord and His mercy toward Israel: "But they rebelled, and vexed his holy Spirit: therefore he was turned to be their enemy, and he fought against them" (Isa. 63:10 KJV). It's difficult to imagine, but it's true. The Holy Ghost can be tormented by human beings.

In the original language, to vex carries the meaning of wearing down, troubling, even afflicting. Only a person can become the target of such torments.

A strong wind cannot be quieted, but the Holy Spirit can: "And He called to me, and spoke to me, saying, 'See, those . . . have given rest to My Spirit'" (Zech. 6:8). The Holy Spirit is a person who responds to your wishes. You can tell Him to be quiet and He will. But then you run the risk of grieving Him.

So many times in public meetings, I have seen the Holy Spirit about to speak and then quieted by some fleshly manifestation. At such sacred moments I have felt the Holy Spirit withdrawing.

The Holy Spirit is not a fighter; He's a lover. If you resist Him,

He will just leave. He's not like Satan, who the Bible says will "flee" from you if you resist him. The Holy Spirit will not run away in fear, but rather He will leave your presence with a wounded heart. If He is grieved, He will gently retreat. If He is quenched, he will quietly depart. How tragic to think that people would vex or attempt to quiet such a lovely person. But they do. The Children of Israel did. And today while He is still longing for our love and our fellowship, we wound Him through our ignorance and rebellion.

I can still hear Kathryn Khulman in Pittsburgh sobbing with such agony: "Please! Don't wound Him. He's all I've got."

SEVEN

Wind for Your Sails

If you ever see a drunk man on the same side of the road, cross over to the other side." That's the advice my father gave the Hinn kids when I was growing up in the Holy Land.

Every morning my brothers and sisters walked with me to the Catholic school. And sure enough it happened—more than once. Almost by instinct, without a word we remembered Daddy's advice and walked on the other side of the street until we were well past the drunken man.

How did we know he was intoxicated? Well, we didn't walk up to him and say, "Mister, are you drunk?" Or "Let me smell your breath!" Of course not. Even as children we knew he was inebriated. Everything about him told us—the way he moved, the look on his face, his disheveled clothes. As they say in England, he was "three sheets to the wind."

The truth about his ungodly behavior was simply this: He was being controlled by the wrong power. He had surrendered to the wrong influence.

The apostle Paul could not have been more blunt when he

said, "Do not be drunk with wine, in which is dissipation; but be filled with the Spirit" (Eph. 5:18). What a contrast between riotous living and righteous living. Drunkenness, Paul warns, brings ungodly actions. But if man or a woman can be controlled by alcohol, how much more can the Holy Spirit control a man or a woman?

Is it difficult to determine who's in control? Not at all. Every day you meet people whose minds and hearts are light-years away from God. It's obvious. You hear it in their language. You see it in their actions. It's as though Satan himself is guiding every movement of their lives.

The Spirit-Filled Life

But what about the person who has had an encounter with the Holy Spirit? What are the outward signs of the Spirit-filled life? There are many, and the transformation is startling. It's beyond explanation. Suddenly positive "manifestations" begin to multiply at every turn.

Just after he says, "Be filled with the Spirit," Paul describes four distinct results you can expect. It is like planting seeds in the soil of the Spirit and reaping a heavenly harvest.

You'll Be Changed

The first manifestation you can expect of a Spirit-filled life is this: *Your speech will be different.* The apostle said we should speak "to one another in psalms" (Eph. 5:19). Can you imagine what an incredible world it would be if our conversation resembled what we read in the Psalms?

A recent study showed that of all the words in the English language, the word used most often is *I*. But the Spirit-led Christian has a new vocabulary. It is not self-centered. It is God-centered. Suddenly you are saying, "Praise the LORD" (Ps. 150:1) and "Let everything that has breath praise the LORD" (v. 6).

Here's the second sign Paul says you should expect: *You'll have a new song.* He says you will be "singing and making melody in your heart to the Lord" (Eph. 5:19). It's much more than a new song—it's a change that takes place in your heart. When you have been transformed on the inside, a melody will bubble up. It's a spontaneous reaction. I don't claim to be a singer, but I've had a song on my lips since the moment I met the Holy Spirit.

The third manifestation is that *you'll start giving thanks:* "Giving thanks always for all things to God the Father in the name of our Lord Jesus Christ" (v. 20). Suddenly you will begin to thank Him for everything. You'll thank Him for the good, and for the not-so-good. You recognize that the Giver of every gift knows exactly what you need. The result is a transformation of your attitude. No matter what happens, you'll say, "Thank you."

The fourth obvious sign is that *you'll become a servant.* Paul says, "Submitting to one another in the fear of God" (v. 21). That's what "honoring one another in love" is all about. Your heart will yearn to help people. The Holy Spirit brings you to the place where you'll say, "Just let me know—I'll do it!"

What does it mean to be "filled with the Spirit"? Some people think it is exactly the same as driving a Honda into a service station and filling the tank with fuel. But that's not it at all.

In my pulpit I have a bottle of oil. I use it, just as the Scripture directs me, to anoint those who come for healing. It is a simple little container, and it is filled with olive oil. But when I use it up, it's gone. The bottle doesn't fill itself up again.

The words "be filled" in Ephesians have no connection to a bottle or a vessel being filled. The Greek present tense is used to tell you that the filling of the Spirit is not a once-and-for-all experience. It's a *continuing* experience.

Have you ever spent a day on a sailboat? It's a great thrill. What happens to the boat when the sails are filled? The ship begins to move. That's what Paul is telling you. He wants you to be filled, not like a container that has no action but like a sail that continues to be filled with wind. Over and over again. He wants you to move forward with the never-ending breeze of the Spirit filling your spiritual sails.

"Who Do You Think You Are?"

Being filled with the Holy Spirit causes action. It happens in your speech, in your heart, in your attitude, and in your activity. What a change! Now your words are uplifting, there's a harmony in your heart, you give thanks to the Lord, and you truly and humbly serve people.

How can a man or a woman who is filled with the Spirit speak with profanity? How can he or she have a heart filled with jealousy, bitterness, and criticism? A Spirit-filled person doesn't say, "Who do you think you are, telling me what to do?" Or "How can God treat me that way?" These are signs of a self-centered person who is "Spirit empty," not "Spirit filled."

When Christ returned to the Father, He did not intend for you to make it on your own. Help was on the way! After all, it is not *your* power or *your* strength that's important: "'Not by might nor by power, but by My Spirit,' says the LORD of hosts" (Zech. 4:6).

It's by the Spirit that you are able to glorify Jesus. It's by the Spirit that your heart is filled with song. It's by the Spirit that you are able to say, "Jesus, I thank you for everything." And it's by the Spirit that you are empowered to say, "I forgive you."

How is the love of God "shed abroad in our hearts"? By the Holy Spirit.

You've never seen the wind, but you have certainly seen the results of the wind. The tree bends. The flag waves. And the ship begins to move. Oh, the force of it.

You don't have to see the Holy Spirit to know that He is alive. You can *feel* the evidence in the power He gives you. Once He fills you, seeking a confirmation is an exercise in futility. A man once asked: "Benny, tell me. Am I filled with the Spirit?"

I said, "Brother, if you don't know, then you're *not!*" You don't have to ask when you see the results. Those who question their infilling have never received it.

It Starts with Salvation

You may ask, "How do I become filled with the Holy Spirit? If I speak in tongues, is that the sign?"

The Holy Spirit is present from the moment you ask the Lord Jesus Christ to forgive your sin and cleanse your heart. If you do not believe that, you don't understand the Trinity. As Paul wrote to Titus, "He saved us, through the washing of regeneration and renewing of the Holy Spirit, whom He poured out on us abundantly through Jesus Christ our Savior, that having been justified by His grace we should become heirs according to the hope of eternal life" (Titus 3:5–7).

But now we are talking about the infilling of the Holy Spirit with the evidence that has been experienced by literally hundreds of millions of people worldwide. The statistics are overwhelming. I know that some still like to argue the point, but *a man with an experience is never at the mercy of a man with an argument.*

I'll never forget the first few days after I was born again. I was like a little kid—and you know what they say about babies. They're always falling, crying, and asking for help. That was me. In fact, I shared with a man in the church the same doubt I've heard many times since. I said, "Oh, I'm so torn up."

He asked, "What's wrong?"

I said, "I'm not sure if I've been filled with the Spirit." I wasn't.

So he said, "Benny, did you ask?"

I answered "Yes, sir."

He said, "That's all you need to do."

Well, you see, I was a babe in Christ. I didn't know what I know now. I truly did not know what I was seeking, but I heard someone say, "If you speak in tongues, that's all you need."

As I learned later, speaking in tongues is only *one* of the gifts. It is not the gifts you need as much as the *giver*. Paul wrote to the church at Rome, "For the gifts and the calling of God are irrevocable" (Rom. 11:29). The gifts will never leave but the giver's power can be withdrawn—and will be withdrawn if the giver is neglected and grieved.

Never forget what happened to King Saul. The Lord said, "I greatly regret that I have set up Saul as king, for he has turned back from following Me, and has not performed My commandments" (1 Sam. 15:11). And as David was being anointed by Samuel to become the new king, "The Spirit of the LORD departed from Saul" (1 Sam. 16:14).

Surrender

Have You Mended Your Sails?

You may ask, "How should I approach the Spirit? How can I become ready to receive Him?"

Perhaps I should ask you a question or two. Is your ship ready to sail? Is it seaworthy? Have you mended the sails? Are they ready to receive the wind of the Spirit when He begins to breathe on you?

It's like preparing for marriage. You spend time in thought and preparation for that moment you stand before the sacred altar. Then you make a vow "to have and to hold from this day forward." You actually *give* yourself to your spouse. It's an unselfish act of loving surrender. And from that time forward a unique bond of fellowship is created and is known only to a husband and wife.

But what happens when you take back part of yourself that was committed in marriage? "You can't have that! It's mine!" And what if your spouse says the same? It would create a barrier in your relationship. The union would begin to crumble. The fellowship would begin to falter. Only total surrender brings total communion. It produces love and understanding.

There is only one way to restore a broken relationship. Like the sail on a vessel, you cannot remain strained and uptight. Just the opposite, you must be flexible and *yield*—actually surrender to a new infilling of love.

The moment you surrender to the Lord, He will fill you with His Spirit. You don't need to beg for the infilling. And it doesn't require a bucket of tears. All it takes is a total surrender to Christ and a willingness to embrace His precious Holy Spirit.

Total surrender brings total infilling, and total submission brings total fellowship. But just as in marriage, you've got to work at it every day: "Jesus, I love you"; "Father God, I adore you"; "precious Holy Spirit, I long for your fellowship." If you neglect communicating just one day, the next time it's a little harder.

Like a Sharp Knife

What happens to a marriage when one partner ignores the other? After a short period of time bitterness begins to enter the heart. Words begin to cut like a sharp knife. Soon the animosity turns to anger, jealousy, and even worse. For many it results in separation, divorce, and hatred. But the rift can so easily be mended. All it takes is a fresh surrender that comes from your very soul. And a renewing of the vow to "love, honor, and cherish."

The same thing will happen if you neglect the Lord. You will develop bitterness and anger. Suddenly you will be out of fellowship with the Lord. That's what happened to the children of Israel in the wilderness. They began to complain, "If only we had died in the land of Egypt! Or if only we had died in this wilderness! Why has the LORD brought us to this land to fall by the sword?" (Num. 14:2–3). And the Lord said to Moses and Aaron, "How long shall I bear with this evil congregation who murmur against Me?" (v. 27).

The children of Israel went from saying, "The Lord is God," to complaining, "Wouldn't it be better to return to Egypt?" What caused the change? They stopped seeking Him, and their hearts became hardened. And before they understood what was happening, they had forsaken Him.

Don't let a day go by without a fresh surrender to the Lord. Paul wrote, "Even though our outward man is perishing, yet the inward man is being renewed day by day" (2 Cor. 4:16). Surrender must be continual, a never-ending emptying of self to the Lord. And once you make it a habit, you'll begin to experience God's perfect union, perfect fellowship, perfect understanding, and perfect love.

I believe it is God's will for you to be *continually* filled with the Holy Spirit. Almost in the same breath that Paul says "Be filled with the Spirit," he says, "Do not be unwise, but understand what the will of the Lord is" (Eph. 5:17). Paul leaves no doubt that it is the Father's will that the Holy Spirit should abide in every believer. It's God's will for every mother, for every father, for every young person—and for you.

Relax, Relax

In a church near Toronto I remember seeing a young man praying to receive the infilling of the Spirit. I'll never forget the look on his face—strained and tense. He was literally begging and begging for an encounter with the Holy Spirit.

I walked over to him and said, "Young man, you won't get anything by begging. Just relax. It's so easy when you surrender." That's what he did, and almost instantly the Spirit came upon him. It was beautiful. A smile came over his face as he began to pray in a heavenly language.

How do you remember? It will never happen if you "try to." It's like learning to swim. If you struggle to swim you'll begin to sink, and you may even drown. That's why the swimming instructor first teaches a child to relax and learn to float. Swimming comes naturally when you don't fight it.

And that's the way it is with surrender—it comes instinctively to a yielded heart. When you met your mate for life, you didn't "try to" fall in love. It's something that is either there or not. You don't have to work at it because love surrenders.

When Jesus is your Lord, when you love Him with all your heart, it's not difficult to surrender to Him. It's the same with the Holy Spirit. Every day when you present yourself to Him, He fills you again. You remain fresh as a flower in the morning sun. He continues to give you life—and the blossoms never seem to fade.

I can't tell you how to approach Him, but here is what I do. So many times I enter my room, lock the door, and just stand there with my arms raised toward heaven. He knows I love Him; I know He loves me. And I am waiting with open arms to receive Him.

Now there was a time years ago that I questioned His love. I'll never, never forget that. It was during a time I was having tremendous struggles with my family. My mom and dad were not born again, and there was such pain in our relationship. Then one night in my room I looked up and said, "Jesus, I know You say in Your Word You love me . . . but please do me a favor. *Tell me* that You love me." And I went to sleep.

In the middle of the night I awakened by a voice that sounded like rushing waters. I can only describe it as a sound that was thick and heavy. Then an audible voice—coming from nowhere yet coming from everywhere at once—began to speak. Above the torrent of water I heard a voice as clear as any I have ever heard saying, "I love you! I love you!" It was the voice of Jesus. At that moment the walls of my room actually seemed to be shaking. I was frightened because the presence of the Lord was so unusual.

But since that moment I have never questioned His love. I believe He gives us such experiences when we need them—not when we want them.

Many times I stand in my room and don't say a word. I keep total silence. I'm sure you have experienced times when you didn't have to utter a word to assure someone of your love. There are special times between two people that if just one sound were made, an unforgettable moment would be destroyed. Quietness is often the best language.

So many times I have stood in my room and suddenly tears have filled my eyes. An unexplainable warmth and beauty fill the air as He begins to fill me afresh. How did it happen? What did I do? Really, I did nothing but just stand in His presence with an inward surrender. But what started in perfect quietness continued with worship and adoration that I never wanted to end.

When you are continually filled by the Spirit of God, your prayer life takes on a dimension you never thought possible. To experience the refreshing breeze of the Spirit that fills your heart with praise, you need to understand how to approach the throne of God in prayer.

Step by Step

There are seven distinct steps to prayer.

The first step is *confession*. Begin by acknowledging who God is. Abram called him, "the LORD, God Most High, the Possessor of heaven and earth" (Gen. 14:22). Begin by declaring the power of the Almighty. Elijah began his prayer on Mount Carmel, "LORD God of Abraham, Isaac, and Israel" (1 Kings 18:36). If you want the fire to fall, begin by confessing who God is.

The next level of prayer is *supplication*. Simply, "Let your request be made known to the Lord." Unfortunately, this is the step on which many people spend far too much time. Their entire prayer life seems to be concentrated on needs, wants, and desires. Of course your personal problems are worthy of God's attention, but when you have shared them, it's not time to say "Amen." The best is yet to come.

The third step—and one that I dearly love—is *adoration*. It should be a time for absolute beauty and worship. Loving Him. Adoring Him. It may begin with the words, "Jesus, I love you." Suddenly you feel the presence of the Holy Spirit, and two hours later you look at your watch and say, "I can't believe the time has gone so fast." It's so real, so alive.

Fourth, there is a time of *intimacy*. It is almost too loving, too sacred, too beautiful to describe. There have been times when, deep in prayer, I felt as if someone was standing there, rubbing my forehead. It was as if the Lord were saying to me, "Thank you. I'm so glad to be with you."

Remember, the Holy Spirit will never force Himself on you.

He doesn't place demands and stipulations on your prayer life. But if you say, "Help me pray," He is ready to respond.

At times in my life my prayer at this level has continued for hours. But intimacy is not a place you can begin. Nor is it possible to rush through the early steps to arrive at this point.

The fifth level of prayer is *intercession*. Jesus said the Spirit would reveal things to us, and that is what happened to me. When you invite the Spirit to help you pray, He does not focus on your selfish needs and wants. No! The focus is outward. He has placed the names and faces of people before me that I had not thought of in years. And I interceded in prayer for them.

But don't believe that it is a period of joy and worship. Just the opposite. The first time I moved into intercession I wasn't sure I wanted it. The communion left. The closeness left. During these times I have felt pain and agony that is difficult to put into words. I have literally pounded the floor with every ounce of my strength as I prayed for my family, for friends, for ministers—even for nations.

Let me warn you. It is possible to move into intercession with a snap of the finger. It does not come instantly because it is a partnership with God that requires a deep and intensely personal relationship. You see, the Holy Spirit leads your prayer life step by step. With me, it did not happen on the first day, or the second, or the third. It was at least six months before I was moving into the depths of prayer. Scripture teaches that if we are faithful with the little things, God will give us more. That's what He does. He's the perfect Father. The perfect teacher.

But what happened next was worth the travail. The sixth step in prayer is *thanksgiving*. As Paul wrote, "But thanks be to God, who gives us the victory through our Lord Jesus Christ" (1 Cor. 15:57). I always spend time giving thanks to the Father, to the Son, and to the Holy Spirit.

Finally, step seven in prayer is *praise*. Sometimes I sing. Sometimes I speak in a Spirit language. But from the depths of my being I burst forth into total praise. It is the purest form of prayer I've ever experienced.

You may ask, "Benny, do you always include all seven steps?" My answer is "Yes!" And here's what's so wonderful about the Spirit: If you allow Him to work through you in prayer, you'll discover that you are not doing much of the praying. He seems to be doing it all. Even in intercession, as painful as it is, the arms of the Spirit are lifting you up, giving instant refreshing when your praying is through.

Paul was right when he said, "praying always with all prayer and supplication in the Spirit" (Eph. 6:18). He knew there was more than one kind of prayer.

"He's Here!"

There is no substitute for the filling of the Spirit that comes as a direct result of your prayer life. It is the power that will affect everything you do.

Recently I was invited to speak in Colombia, South America. It was a three-day crusade, and on the evening of the second day, Wednesday, I was speaking on the Holy Spirit. In the middle of my message I felt the power of the Holy Spirit move over the service. I felt His presence, stopped preaching, and told the people, "He's here!" Ministers on the platform and people in the audience felt the same thing—it was like a gust of wind that entered and swirled inside that place.

People stood to their feet in a spontaneous outburst of praise. But they didn't stand long. All over, people began to collapse and fall to the floor under the power of the Holy Ghost. They were "slain" in the Spirit.

What happened next was exactly what I have seen repeated in services all over the world. People began to receive Christ as their personal Savior, and healings began to take place across the auditorium.

When I speak about the Holy Spirit an unusual anointing follows the teaching. Always. There is an incredible manifestation of God's presence—very different from at any other time. The miracles seem to be more intense. A greater number of people are saved than in other meetings. The touch of God on people's lives is more pronounced.

In those services the altar calls seem to be so easy. There's no begging or pleading. Instantly, people flock to the front for salvation. Just as the Lord promised, the Spirit draws people to Christ.

After the services people come up to say, "This was the most powerful meeting I have ever been in!" It's as if the Holy Spirit has honored the service because He is such a welcomed guest.

During that same crusade, Pastor Colin, my interpreter, came to me just after a morning teaching session on the Holy Spirit with nearly two thousand preachers. He began to sob. Then he lifted his head from his hands and said with great emotion, "Dear Brother, I know so little about the Holy Spirit. I feel like I'm in kindergarten." He was overcome with the reality of the message.

At other times I've seen an interpreter stop right in the middle of my message and begin to cry uncontrollably. That's the power of the Spirit.

What happens in a service can happen to you right where you are. That's why I am asking you to surrender totally to the Spirit. You'll begin to understand what Paul means when he says: "Be filled with the Spirit . . . speaking to one another in psalms . . . singing and making melody in your heart to the Lord, giving thanks always . . . to God the Father." And you'll know why he says, "Submit to one another" (Eph. 5:18–21).

A Second Wind

Are you ready for God's heavenly breeze to fill your sails? It starts with salvation when you confess your sin and commit your life to follow Jesus as Lord and Savior. Even Christ talked about the wind when He talked about redemption. He told Nicodemus, a member of the Jewish ruling council, "Do not marvel that I said to you, 'You must be born again.' The wind blows where it wishes, and you hear the sound of it, but cannot tell where it comes from and where it goes. So is everyone who is born of the Spirit" (John 3:7–8).

Just as salvation is described as a wind, the Holy Spirit is described as a *second wind*—a wind of power. On the day of pentecost, "Suddenly there came a sound from heaven, as of a rushing mighty wind, and it filled the whole house where they were sitting" (Acts 2:2). The wind of the Spirit is rushing, and it is mighty. It is a power that will set your life in motion.

It's time to launch your vessel. Hoist your sail, and begin to be filled—continually filled—with the wind of the Holy Spirit.

EIGHT

A Mighty Entrance

How could it be? I had just given my life to the Lord, and I was struggling to live the Christian life.

When I think about what is happening to me now, it sounds impossible. In February 1972 after my "born again" experience, I knew my heart had been cleansed, but the difficulties I faced seemed insurmountable. There were conflicts at home, indecision about my future, and a self-image as low as the floor beneath my feet.

Oh, how I wrestled with my life! It was even difficult at times to give my total love to the Lord. I had so many urgent questions. Then two weeks later I was filled with the Spirit. I expected heaven on earth from that moment on. But it didn't happen. My day-to-day struggles continued.

Certainly there were great moments of joy and exhilaration. And I would not have traded my spiritual experiences for all the oil in Saudi Arabia. But deep inside there was a gnawing question that haunted me month after month. "Is that all there is?" I wondered. The question would not go away. "Doesn't the Lord have something more for me?"

And then, in the middle of a cold December night nearly two years after I met Christ, it happened. As I lay on my bed in Toronto, the Holy Spirit made a mighty entrance into my room. It felt like a jolt of electricity and a blanket of warmth all at once.

It took me only a few days to realize the significance of what had happened. *My struggle was over!* I had found the simplicity of the Christian life—a personal relationship with the Holy Ghost.

Today, my heart is still troubled, but for an entirely different reason. I am deeply distressed that millions of Christians have never received even a thimbleful of what God has in store for them. They're missing the best part. And they'll never know how marvelous a walk with Christ can really be until they discover the third person of the Trinity. *He's the one who helps us with the struggle.*

No More Wrestling

The moment the Spirit came into my life I no longer had to battle my adversaries. They were still there, but the wrestling and the worry seemed to vanish. What happened to me was the same thing that was spoken to Israel centuries ago through the prophet Ezekiel. Living in a time of political upheaval, he was told by the Lord: "I will give you a new heart and put a new spirit within you; I will take the heart of stone out of your flesh and give you a heart of flesh. I will put My Spirit within you and cause you to walk in My statutes, and you will keep My judgments and do them" (Ezek. 36:26–27).

The problem still exists today! Millions of people are in a daily fight to keep the laws of God, and they are losing the war because they do not understand the Father's battle plan. His strategy could not be more succinct: *"I will put My Spirit within you,"* says the Lord. And why is that His agenda? He wants to "cause you"—from deep inside your heart—to follow His statutes. He wants to make it easy to *keep* His laws.

Do you find it tough to keep God's commandments? Don't feel all alone. It's totally impossible to succeed by yourself, and God doesn't expect you to. You need help! But to whom should you turn? God the Father is in heaven and so is God the Son. You need a friend here and now, and the person of the Trinity that is dwelling on earth is the Holy Spirit. He's the one you desperately need to know.

If you took a survey and asked people what they wanted most from God, the answer would likely be, "I want God to be happy with me." And that's what the Lord promised the prophet Ezekiel. God said, "I will not hide My face from them anymore, for I shall have poured out My Spirit on the house of Israel" (Ezek. 39:29).

The moment the Holy Spirit becomes a part of your life, God will begin to look in your direction. His face will begin to shine on you. The Father's great desire is that you receive Him, be filled with Him, and have fellowship with Him. It makes Him happy.

Just begin to read the book of Acts, and you'll sense what God had planned. The apostles had a tremendous relationship with the Holy Ghost and the evidence is recorded on every page. But perhaps more inspiring is the fact that the "acts" continue to happen—even today. If the miraculous works of the Holy Spirit were all recorded, there wouldn't be a library large enough to contain the volumes.

What transpired in the Upper Room should have been no surprise. Before He ascended to heaven, Jesus Himself told His followers not to leave Jerusalem, but to wait for the gift His Father promised, "which you have heard from Me; for John truly baptized with water, but you shall be baptized with the Holy Spirit not many days from now" (Acts 1:4–5).

Christ even described what it would be like and how it would change their lives: "You shall receive power when the Holy Spirit has come upon you; and you shall be witnesses to Me in Jerusalem, and in all Judea and Samaria, and to the end of the earth" (v.8).

The Spirit's Arrival

A Violent Wind

Just as real as the coming of Jesus to earth, so was the coming of the Holy Ghost. Just as the prophets predicted the Messiah, so did they foretell the coming of the Spirit. Hundreds of years before Christ, God told Joel,

> I will pour out My Spirit on all flesh;
> Your sons and your daughters shall prophesy,
> Your old men shall dream dreams,
> Your young men shall see visions;
> And also on My menservants and on My maidservants
> I will pour out My Spirit in those days. (Joel 2:28–29)

The Holy Spirit came. And *what a mighty entrance!* The sound of a thunderous wind. Tongues of fire. A demonstration of God's power. His arrival on earth was nothing short of spectacular!

> When the Day of Pentecost had fully come, they were all with one accord in one place. And suddenly there came from heaven, a sound of a rushing mighty wind, and it filled the whole house where they were sitting. Then there appeared to them divided tongues, as of fire, and one sat upon each of them. And they were all filled with the Holy Spirit and began to speak with other tongues, as the Spirit gave them utterance. (Acts 2:1–4)

It was exactly as Isaiah had foretold: "With stammering lips and another tongue He will speak . . ." (Isa. 28:11).

Now when Jesus was born, the moment was marked by peace and quietness. It was a beautiful night in Bethlehem, so clear that the shepherds followed the star to the manger. What a contrast to the powerful noise that accompanied the arrival of the Holy Spirit. It created such a clamor in Jerusalem that "When this sound occurred, the multitude came together, and were confused" (Acts 2:6).

I used to think the phrase "When it was noised abroad" meant that someone was running around the city saying, "Come and see what is happening!" But that's not the case. The pandemonium of what happened literally was heard all over town. You see, "There were dwelling in Jerusalem Jews, devout men, from every nation under heaven" (v. 5). Can you imagine what they thought?

The Word says that when they heard this sound they rushed to the scene in bewilderment "because everyone heard them speak in his own language" (v. 6).

Utterly amazed, they asked: "Are not all these who speak Galileans? And how is it that we hear, each in our own native language?" (vv. 7–8). And when they heard them declare the wonders of God in their own tongues, they asked each other, "What could this mean?" (v. 12).

Why 120?

His thunderous coming was not scheduled for a temple made of stone. Instead, the Holy Spirit came upon 120 believers who became the new temple of God.

Do you recall that when Solomon finished his temple he had "one hundred and twenty priests sounding trumpets" (2 Chron. 5:12)? Scripture records that "The house of the LORD, was filled with a cloud, so that the priests could not continue ministering because of the cloud; for the glory of the LORD filled the house of God" (vv.13–14).

It happened again in the Upper Room. One hundred and twenty came together and the Spirit of God filled the temple. Why 120? It is the number of the closing of the age of the flesh and the opening of the age of the Spirit. In Genesis, where for 120 years, Noah was building the ark, the age of the flesh ended. God said, "My Spirit shall not strive with man forever, for he is indeed flesh; yet his days shall be one hundred and twenty years" (Gen. 6:3).

It is precisely for this purpose that the Lord gathered 120 at pentecost. So that God the Holy Spirit could be released among the nations. *It marked the beginning of the age of the Spirit.*

Observers couldn't understand what was happening! Some made fun of them and said, "They are full of new wine" (Acts 2:13). But Peter "standing up with the eleven, raised his voice and said to them, 'Men of Judea and all who dwell in Jerusalem, let this be known to you, and heed my words. For these are not drunk, as you suppose, since it is only the third hour of the day. But this is what was spoken by the prophet Joel'" (v. 14–16).

The 120 were so filled with the Spirit that they could not stand under their own power. The Spirit was so mighty that He took control over the actions of the believers. He was at work changing their speech, their emotions, and their behavior. What Jerusalem witnessed was not drunkenness, but the incredible joy that comes when the Spirit takes control. I've been accused of a few things myself.

What a transformation in timid Peter. It brought out the "preacher" in him as he "raised his voice" and spoke with boldness to the growing crowd. But who do you think gave him the words? The captivating message was that of the Holy Ghost. "For our gospel did not come to you in word only, but also in power, and in the Holy Spirit" (1 Thess. 1:5). That's right. The gospel is preached by the Holy Spirit. Remember, the Word says, the Spirit "working with them." He's the one who does the work.

Now watch what begins to happen suddenly in the book of Acts. *The Holy Spirit gives tremendous authority to those who have received Him.* It's three o'clock in the afternoon as Peter and John were going up to the temple, and "a certain man lame from his mother's womb was carried, whom they laid daily at the gate of the temple which is called Beautiful, to ask alms from those who entered the temple" (Acts 3:2).

Turning to the disheveled beggar, "fixing his eyes on him, with John, Peter said, 'Look at us'" (v. 4). It's a marvelous thing to see a man completely given over to the Holy Spirit. Peter was filled with a boldness and power he had never known as he looked deep into the soul of this poor man—right through his eyes.

The beggar knew Peter and John were not playing games. A holy boldness had been vested in the apostles. When Peter said, "Look at us," the man immediately "gave them his attention, expecting to receive something from them" (v. 5).

Then Peter said, "Silver and gold I do not have, but what I do have I give you: In the name of Jesus Christ of Nazareth, rise up and walk" (v. 6). He took him by the right hand, helped him up, and instantly the man's feet and ankles became strong. "So he, leaping up, stood and walked and entered the temple with them—walking, leaping, and praising God" (vv. 7–8).

Can you imagine the consternation in the temple? The beggar made a mighty entrance of his own. They recognized him immediately and "were filled with wonder and amazement at what had happened to him" (v. 10).

Not a "Yesterday" Experience

The power and authority the apostles received began to touch lives at every turn. Their ministry was followed by "many signs and wonders . . . among the people" (Acts 5:12). And what was the result? "Believers were increasingly added to the Lord, multitudes of both men and women" (v. 14). *The signs that followed the coming of the Holy Spirit led people directly to Christ.* That's an important fact to remember.

What happened in the Upper Room was not a one-time experience, nor a footnote of history. The Spirit-filled believers established an ongoing relationship with the Holy Ghost. They *continued* to be filled. When Peter was called before the Sanhedrin over the healing of the beggar, they asked "By what power or by what name have you done this?" Peter was "filled with the Holy Spirit" when he spoke (Acts 4:7–8). Not past tense, but *present* tense. "Filled" describes the apostle at that very moment.

Over and over in Scripture, when followers of Christ are portrayed as "filled with the Spirit," the reference is to a new infilling, not to something that happened yesterday or last month.

Peter was so full of the Spirit in the temple that he had authority over his critics. Undaunted, he said: "Rulers of the people and elders of Israel: If we this day are judged for a good deed done to a helpless man, by what means he has been made well, let it be known to you all, and to all the people of Israel, that by the name of Jesus Christ of Nazareth, whom you crucified, whom God raised from the dead, by Him this man stands here before you whole" (Acts 4:8–10).

Do you realize that the power of the Spirit can so infill you that you fear absolutely no one? It's possible to establish such a communion with Him that even addressing the leader of a nation would cause no apprehension. The Spirit will lift your head, square your shoulders, and instill in you an unexpected confidence.

When I traveled to the Vatican in Rome to meet the pope, I thought I would be nervous. But it didn't happen because I was so full of my subject. And among the Vatican leaders I sensed a hunger for things of the Spirit.

Peter the Mighty

Peter was facing more than the priests of the temple. He was actually up against the government of Israel. In fact the night before he was permitted to address the priests, he and John were thrown in jail. But when he spoke, the words were hard-hitting. He told them the Lord was "the 'stone which was rejected by you builders, which has become the chief cornerstone'" (Acts 4:11). It was a direct quotation of Psalm 118:22.

Was this the same Peter who, a few weeks before, in the same place, before the same people, had been cowed by the sneer of a girl and had denied his Master? Now here he was, filled with the Spirit, in utter fearlessness, defying the murderers of Jesus.

It was no longer Peter the meek. It was Peter the mighty. What a change the Spirit made!

So great was this fellowship with the Holy Ghost that Peter directly challenged Ananias. He said: "Ananias, why has Satan filled your heart to lie to the Holy Spirit?" (Acts 5:3). Peter's words and God's actions were so forceful that "great fear came upon all those who heard these things" (v. 5).

His Closeness to Us

I can tell you from personal experience that there comes a point where fellowship of the Spirit becomes so real, so deep, and so great that your words and actions conform to *His* words and actions. When you know, for example, that He has been grieved, you can speak boldly on His behalf, knowing He is flowing through you at that very moment. You will be so near to Him that you will actually feel Him responding to what you have said.

I believe the day is approaching when men and women of God will become so close to the Spirit of God that we will witness much more than healings and miracles. We will witness the Spirit as He scatters those who dare to fight Him.

Never forget Ananias. He "fell down and breathed his last" (Acts 5:5). And never forget Gehazi. He lied to Elisha about the gifts Naaman brought to him. Naaman was healed, but the Spirit led Elisha to say, "The leprosy of Naaman shall cling to you and your descendants forever" (2 Kings 5:27). And that is exactly what happened.

Jesus made a very powerful statement when He said, " 'As the Father has sent Me, I also send you.' And when He had said this, He breathed on them, and said to them, 'Receive the Holy Spirit. If you forgive the sins of any, they are forgiven them; if you retain the sins of any, they are retained' " (John 20:21–23). This must have been a sobering thought and not one to be taken lightly by the apostles.

The Face of an Angel

Peter was so close to the Spirit he told his accusers, "We are His witnesses to these things, and so also is the Holy Spirit whom God has given to those who obey Him" (Acts 5:32).

The Holy Ghost so possessed Stephen that when he was brought before the priests, "all who sat in the council, looking steadfastly at him, saw his face as the face of an angel" (Acts 6:15). But, oh, the words he spoke. "You stiff-necked . . . in heart and ears! You always resist the Holy Spirit; as your fathers did, so do you" (Acts 7:51). Why did he say that? Because of what he was *filled* with: "But he, being full of the Holy Spirit, gazed into heaven and saw the glory of God, and Jesus standing at the right hand of God" (v. 55).

The presence of the Spirit became so powerful in Stephen's life that he was able to look up and see God's glory. He even took on the emotions and attributes of the Spirit as he was being stoned. Stephen said, "Lord, do not charge them with this sin" (Acts 7:60). Can you imagine such a reaction? He didn't say to God, "Judge them. Kill them. Slay them." The Holy Spirit made the difference.

I am convinced there is a point in your relationship with the Spirit when the anointing becomes so heavy on you—His presence so close to you—that you can look up and see a vision of God. That's how real He can become.

Saul, during his dramatic conversion, had a firsthand experience with the awesome power of the Holy Ghost. As he was on his way to Damascus, breathing out murderous threats against the followers of Christ, "suddenly a light shone around him from heaven. Then he fell to the ground, and heard a voice saying to him, 'Saul, Saul, why are you persecuting Me?'" (Acts 9:3–4).

He was trembling and astonished. "Who are You, Lord?" Saul asked. "I am Jesus, whom you are persecuting," He replied. "Arise and go into the city, and you will be told what you must do" (Acts 9:5–6). The men traveling with Saul were stunned and speechless. Saul was blinded by the experience for three days before God healed him and he was "filled with the Holy Spirit" (v. 17).

Again the Spirit made a mighty entrance. He transformed Saul the antagonist into Paul the apostle. In fact, the effect was felt across the land. The church throughout Judea, Galilee, and Samaria "had peace and were edified. And walking in the fear of the Lord and in the comfort of the Holy Spirit, they were multiplied" (Acts 9:31).

I can only imagine what would happen if every minister in the land were to fall prostrate and seek a personal relationship with the Holy Spirit. Talk about revival! I believe it would so revolutionize the church world that the sanctuaries could not begin to accommodate the people.

Thank God for pastors who are "alive" in the Spirit, but I've heard some ministers that, to be honest, would be better suited as morticians! A continuing communion with the Spirit makes the difference. People are starving for a reality that only the Holy Ghost makes possible.

He Never Stops Working

From the moment of pentecost the Spirit began His work on earth, and it has never stopped. Never! It's incredible how He intervened in the life of Peter. As he was praying on a rooftop, God gave him a vision, and "while Peter thought about the vision, the Spirit said to him, 'Behold, three men are seeking you. Arise therefore, go down and go with them, doubting nothing; for I have sent them" (Acts 10:19–20).

The three men the Spirit told him about were sent by a God-fearing man named Cornelius, a centurion in the Italian regiment. He also had a vision: "He saw clearly . . . an angel of God coming in and saying to him . . . 'Now send men to Joppa, and send for Simon whose surname is Peter'" (Acts 10:3, 5). But it was not the angel speaking. It was the Holy Spirit speaking *through* the angel. Remember? The "Spirit said . . . I have sent them" (vv. 19–20).

The Holy Spirit is an active person. He never stops working. He'll even send an angel to you if that is what you have need of. What happens on earth is the *Spirit's* doing. He's the representative of the Father and the Son.

At the house of Cornelius, Peter preached the death, burial, and resurrection of Christ. And "while Peter was still speaking these words, the Holy Spirit fell upon all those who heard the word" (Acts 10:44). The believers who had come with him, "were astonished . . .

because the gift of the Holy Spirit had been poured out on the Gentiles also. For they heard them speak with tongues and magnify God" (vv. 45–46). Never forget that *the Word comes first.* The message of Christ takes preeminence. The gospel is the foundation for everything God the Holy Spirit was sent to do.

The Spirit is concerned about your life—even your future. He wants to guide you, protect you, even warn you of what lies ahead. You ask, "Can the Holy Spirit prophesy about things to come?" Look at what happened when Barnabas went to the great city of Antioch. Over half a million people lived there at the time. For an entire year Barnabas and Saul taught great numbers of people in that growing megachurch.

> And in these days prophets came from Jerusalem to Antioch. Then one of them, named Agabus, stood up and showed by the Spirit that there was going to be a great famine throughout all the world, which also happened in the days of Claudius Caesar. Then the disciples, each according to his ability, determined to send relief to the brethren dwelling in Judea. (Acts 11: 27–29)

That's how close the Holy Spirit was to their daily lives. He revealed a coming drought and thus allowed them to be prepared when the famine actually came. The Spirit is a *person*, and He's deeply concerned about *people*. He knows what is happening in your life and has great concern for you.

The Spirit and the Sorcerer

Isn't it time that you allow the Spirit to order your steps? Why attempt to plan your own course when He knows every inch of the road ahead, every dangerous curve, every pothole. That's what the Christians at Antioch learned. "As they ministered to the Lord and fasted, the Holy Spirit said, 'Now separate to Me Barnabas and Saul for the work to which I have called them'" (Acts 13:2). They responded immediately: "So, being sent out by the Holy Spirit, they went down to Seleucia, and from there they sailed to Cyprus" (v. 4).

The disciples were doing the work of the Father, but who sent them? They received direct instructions from the Spirit. And during their journey the Holy Ghost never stopped working. He even gave them power over a false prophet.

Elymas was a Jewish sorcerer and a magician. He tried to stop what the power of God was doing on Cyprus. But, "Saul, who also is called Paul, filled with the Holy Spirit, looked intently at [Elymas] and said, 'O full of all deceit and all fraud, you son of the devil, you enemy of all righteousness, will you not cease perverting the straight ways of the Lord?'" (Acts 13:9–10).

What an indictment! In fact, the Spirit was so strong on Paul that he told the sorcerer he would become blind. And he did. But as a direct result people began turning to Christ, "and the word of the Lord was being spread throughout all the region" (Acts 13:49). "And the disciples were filled with joy and with the Holy Spirit" (v. 52).

You ask, "Should I allow the Holy Spirit to make *all* the decisions? After all, didn't God give me a mind of my own?" Of course He did. But what makes sense to you should also make sense to the Spirit. The church council at Jerusalem wrote, "It seemed good to the Holy Spirit, and to us . . ." (Acts 15:28). When it is right it will be confirmed by the Holy Ghost, and you will know the direction to take.

The Message and the Messenger

If the Spirit was so necessary for Christ, He should be every bit as important to you. Jesus was born of the Spirit, anointed by the

Spirit, cast out devils by the Spirit, received his fullness by the Spirit, and performed miracles by the Spirit. And it was by the Holy Ghost that He taught, gave commands, empowered and governed the church, offered Himself on the cross, and was resurrected.

"How much more shall the blood of Christ, who through the eternal Spirit offered Himself without spot to God, purge your conscience from dead works to serve the living God?" (Heb. 9:14). The same Spirit that was essential for the earthly work of Christ is necessary for you. He is indispensable.

Your experience of salvation is based on Christ, the cross, and your confession. But how did you receive the *reality* of your regeneration? How did you *know* your heart had been cleansed? That, my friend, is the work of the Holy Spirit. It's the Spirit of the Lord that places the message in your very soul. You can't find adequate words to describe or explain it, but you know it is as valid as life itself.

If that reality is so strong, so deep, and so personal, then how real is the one who gives it? It's a significant question. How real must be the messenger if the message is so real?

The Holy Spirit longs for a daily, ongoing personal relationship with you. He wants to make an entrance—*a mighty entrance*—into your life.

NINE

Room for the Spirit

For generations, people have been led to believe that the Spirit is an "it." From a thousand voices, millions of written words, and an attitude that has permeated the Christian faith, we have been programmed to think of the Holy Ghost as a some*thing* rather than as a some*one*.

I heard a chorus recently that said, "Give me more of You!" And I thought, *Why, that's unscriptural.* You can't take a part of Him. He's a person. You can't break Him into little pieces, an arm this week and a leg the next. It's not, "Give me more of you." It's exactly the opposite. You should be crying out to the Spirit, "Please, take more of *me.*" He doesn't surrender to you. No! You surrender to Him.

A Place for Him

Without a doubt, the most overlooked message of the church today is that *the Holy Spirit is real and we must make a place for Him.*

Sad, isn't it. Ministers of the gospel by the thousands do not comprehend the workings of the Spirit on planet earth. I'm afraid they've been programmed, too. From Sunday school to seminary, they have been led to believe that the Spirit is a minor member of the Godhead who came at pentecost and has been floating in the clouds ever since. Many actually avoid speaking His name lest people confuse them with one of those off-the-wall charismatics.

God intended that the church be alive and vibrant. Just before He returned to heaven, Jesus uttered the unforgettable words, "These signs will follow those who believe . . ." (Mark 16:17). Perhaps the most puzzling question I have as a minister is this: *If the Holy Spirit was sent to give Christians power to live a victorious life, why are so many despondent and defeated?*

When I was an evangelist, I went to a church, conducted a rally, prayed for the needs of the people, and returned to my home. I really did not know what was taking place in the daily lives of the people. But now that I am a pastor, my perspective has totally changed. And I am disturbed by what I see.

I now realize that infinitely more people have major problems than I ever dreamed possible. That so many believers are disheartened, dejected, on the verge of spiritual bankruptcy is almost unthinkable. Repeatedly I see tiny problems creep into people's lives and then suddenly emerge as Goliaths, or Mount Everests.

"Father God," I ask, "where is the victory? Where is the joy?"

Just last week our congregation experienced a mighty outpouring of the Spirit on Sunday night. As I ministered to the people, I sensed an unusual anointing. On the way home I was shouting, "Hallelujah!" I said to my wife, Suzanne, "What a great service! Isn't it wonderful what God is doing here?" But just as I walked in the door of our home, the phone rang. And for the next thirty minutes I heard the heartbreaking story of a man who had been in that very service. He cried and cried as he told me, "I just don't know where to turn."

It happens over and over again.

Who's Got the Power?

What's wrong? Why is it that the early church had such power and we have so little of it? With one word they commanded demons to depart, and we seem so fearful and alarmed. Just mention demons, and Christians do the hundred-yard dash. Many pastors won't even talk about them, as if ignoring the topic would drive them out.

It's difficult to understand. Instead of preaching to people that they can be free, many minister keep a silence that leaves many in bondage. Rather than obey the words of Christ, "they shall cast out devils" (Mark 16:17), they tell their people that what is really going on doesn't exist—that's it's all in their minds. And the people murmur, "Lord, I can't find an answer. I can't find help!"

Is it any wonder that some cultists have more power than some Christians? Should we be surprised when satanic followers demonstrate more of the supernatural than many followers of Christ? How is it possible? If God is omnipotent and Satan has such a tiny fraction of power, how can a disciple of the devil operate with any authority?

It's really very simple. A person who uses 100 percent of just a tiny fraction has more power than someone who can tap into the energy of the universe but doesn't even try. I am deeply troubled when I think about a sinner receiving more from Satan than a believer who asks nothing from God can receive.

It's time you begin to exercise the power of the Almighty. You need to know that God is greater than any demon and that only one word from Jesus destroys the devil. Just one of His angels can bind Satan in the pit (Rev. 20: 1–3). God is not weak—His people are.

Here's the only conclusion I have been able to reach. *The reason the church and so many people in it have become so defeated is that it has ignored the most powerful person in the universe—the Holy Spirit.* Again,

" 'Not by might nor by power, but by My Spirit,' says the LORD of hosts" (Zech. 4:6). And the next words are just as exciting: "Who are you, O great mountain? . . . you shall become a plain" (v. 7).

You need more than a Caterpillar tractor to level the mammoth pile of rocks that stands before you. It's a giant mountain of futility and fear. And the excavation you need is only possible through the energizing power of the Holy Spirit.

Real, Not Counterfeit

God, throughout His Word, gives a prescription for breaking the yoke of bondage. He knows exactly what it takes to lift your heavy burden. It is called the *anointing:*

> It shall come to pass in that day
> That his burden will be taken away from your shoulder,
> And his yoke from your neck,
> And the yoke will be destroyed because of the anointing
> oil. (Isa. 10:27)

As God removed Israel's burden, so also will He remove the yoke from you. After all, Satan is the treacherous one that has placed that heavy yoke upon you. But Jesus, who declared that the bondage would be destroyed, said, "My yoke is easy and My burden is light" (Matt. 11:30).

The ever-tightening yoke can be broken by the Spirit. But not just for that moment. It's not a temporary solution. He stays with you, continuing to lift the burden and to guide you on a brand-new path. The apostle John, speaking of the Spirit, wrote, "The anointing which you have received from Him abides in you, and you do not need that anyone teach you; but as the same anointing teaches you concerning all things, and is true, and is not a lie, and just as it has taught you, you will abide in Him" (1 John 2:27).

It doesn't take a Ph.D. to be able to discern who has an anointing and who doesn't. Even an unregenerate sinner flipping a television dial during the Sunday-morning "God slot" knows the touch of the Spirit when he sees it. He recognizes it because, like a diamond, it is so rare.

There is nothing more tragic than people who don't have an anointing trying to produce it. They try to force it, but the touch of the Lord is just not there. How many times have you traveled to hear a great speaker or Bible teacher only to find out that the person is just an empty shell, that there is nothing but knowledge on the inside. Filled with facts and information but absolutely lifeless, they are walking and talking but their words are dead.

I'll never forget what happened at a conference I attended on the west coast. In an afternoon session a young man was introduced to sing. With a tremendous, well-trained voice he sang "The King Is Coming!" All the people enjoyed it, and they gave him a great applause when he had finished.

I don't know how it happened, but in the evening service a lady sang exactly the same song. Frankly, she didn't look like a singer, her voice was a little nasal, and some of the notes were off pitch. But she had something else that made up for those deficiencies a thousand times over. By the time she got to the second chorus, people were on their feet. Their hands were raised to heaven. The power in that place was electric. And it didn't stop when she finished. We praised the Lord and praised Him again. Then we began to applaud—for the longest time. But we weren't giving the singer an ovation. We were applauding the Giver of song.

What made the difference? My friend, *it was the anointing!* It was the power of the Spirit in that lady's life.

During my ministry in Canada, we were one of the sponsoring groups of a Billy Graham crusade. The preparations for the meetings were as organized as anything I'd ever seen. And the services themselves were "tame" compared to what I was used to. But when Graham began to speak, there was an unmistakable touch of the Spirit on his message. The content was Christ, but I could tell I was in the presence of a man who has a deep personal fellowship with the Spirit.

Words That Stunned the Synagogue

Since Creation people have been fascinated by the anointing. It has been marveled at, manifested, and even mimicked. But the true anointing has always been—and still remains—a function of God the Holy Spirit.

What is its purpose? So that you might proclaim the message with power.

> The Spirit of the Lord GOD is upon Me,
> Because the LORD has anointed Me
> To preach good tidings to the poor;
> He has sent Me to heal the brokenhearted,
> To proclaim liberty to the captives,
> And the opening of the prison to those who are bound;
> To proclaim the acceptable year of the LORD . . ." (Isa. 61:1–2)

But those are not just the words of an Old Testament prophet. Jesus quoted them to a stunned audience at the synagogue in Nazareth (Luke 4:18–19).

You must never forget that to understand the Holy Spirit you must know that He is God. That description may seem foreign to you, but it is as basic as the Word itself. He was the power of Creation.

Do you recall the words in the book of Job? "The Spirit of God has made me, and the breath of the Almighty gives me life" (Job 33:4).

While God the Father was in heaven on the throne of Glory saying, "Let us make man," the Holy Spirit was doing His work on earth. Even the second verse states that at Creation "the Spirit of God was hovering over the face of the waters" (Gen. 1:2). And the psalmist, speaking of the creatures on earth, wrote, "You send forth Your Spirit, they are created; and You renew the face of the earth" (Ps. 104:30).

Spiritual Growth

If you want the anointing of the Spirit to become evident in your life, it begins with an understanding of who He is, how He operates, and how you can enter into His fellowship. The Holy Spirit was not sent just to make you feel good. He'll certainly do that, but He is much more. He has equality in the Godhead and deserves our worship just as do God the Father and God the Son. But that is just the start. Your spiritual growth is not different from that of a giant oak tree. It must be fed and nourished.

What Do I Do Next?

Recently a man told me, "Benny, I want to thank you for introducing me to the Holy Spirit in 1978."

I said, "That's great. Tell me what's been happening since?"

His face was a blank as he said, "Well, nothing really. I just remember what it was like when I met Him."

"Why do you think nothing has happened?" I asked.

I'll never forget his reply: "I guess I didn't know what to do."

Perhaps I've expected every person who's been introduced to the Spirit to respond as I did. I literally shut myself away with the

Word and the Spirit and absorbed what He had to offer like a sponge. It took time, hundreds and hundreds of hours with the precious Holy Spirit.

I realize that for many people it's nearly impossible to find the time to search and search the Scriptures. But just by reading this book you are receiving in a succinct manner what it took the Spirit years to share with me. But there is one thing I cannot do for you. I can't wave a spiritual wand over your head and place an anointing on you. That only comes with a personal, deeply private encounter with the Spirit. And it continues and grows with a fellowship and communion that only you can establish.

Your growth in the Spirit will begin the moment you begin to see that the Spirit of God is truly God. I can't repeat it enough because the mental picture of a weak personality has been drilled into our psyche from childhood. I remember seeing a book that said, "The Holy Spirit is a servant to the Body of Christ." That's the kind of error I'm talking about. He's not a servant; He's in charge. He's the *leader* of the body of Christ.

Let me share something I have come to know. The Holy Spirit is not only God; He's also the Father of the Lord Jesus Christ. Before you say, "Now hold it there, Benedictus," let me point you to the Word.

You say, "I thought God the Father was the Father of Jesus." Well, you're right, but you're also wrong. Let me show you why. In the first chapter of the Gospels we are told that the Holy Ghost is the Father of the Lord. "Now the birth of Jesus Christ was as follows: After His mother Mary was betrothed to Joseph, before they came together, she was found with child of the Holy Spirit" (Matt. 1:18).

Even Mary was concerned. Mary said to the angel, "'How can this be, since I do not know a man?' And the angel answered and said to her, 'The Holy Spirit will come upon you, and the power of the Highest will overshadow you; therefore, also, that Holy One who is to be born will be called the Son of God'" (Luke 1:34–35). There you have it. He is called the Son of God, but it was the Holy Spirit that came upon the mother of Christ. That's the closeness of the Trinity—a child of God the Father and a child of God the Spirit in one.

Even the attributes of Jesus were given Him by the Spirit. Speaking of the coming Christ, Isaiah wrote,

> There shall come forth a Rod from the stem of Jesse,
> And a Branch shall grow out of his roots.
> The Spirit of the LORD shall rest upon Him,
> The Spirit of wisdom and understanding,
> The Spirit of counsel and might,
> The Spirit of knowledge and of fear of the LORD. (Isa. 11:1–2)

Who Is the Father?

Jesus Christ is a child of the Spirit. And just as earthly parents love their little baby, so the Holy Ghost loved the Lord. Have you ever seen a proud father hold a newborn in his arms, squeeze it tight, and love it? I think we forget that the Holy Spirit has emotions too. He loves what He has created; that's why He wants to place His arms around *you*.

Can you see God the Father in heaven saying to the Spirit, "Take my Son and make Him flesh"? It was the miracle of miracles. The Holy Spirit took that seed and placed it within Mary's body. But not only was He the Father of the Lord, He was also the one who anointed Him.

Picture, if you will, God the Father sitting on His throne in heaven and Jesus on earth healing the sick and performing miracles. And what about the Holy Ghost? He's the channel, the contact between both personalities. Now the Father picks up the phone (as if He needed one) and says, "Holy Spirit?"

"Yes, Sir," says the Spirit as He picks up the receiver.

God says, "I want you to lead Jesus into the wilderness because I'm going to send the devil to test Him."

The Spirit says, "Yes, Sir," and rushes to Christ. "Jesus, come along with Me," He says.

Do you see how the Holy Spirit is the contact between both personalities?

Or picture this. Jesus is walking past a man who is very sick. Again, the Father picks up the phone and says, "Holy Spirit? Stop Jesus! Tell Him to halt right where He is."

The Spirit says, "Okay. Jesus, stop."

He speaks into the phone and says, "Father, what should He do?"

"Tell Him to heal that man," says the voice of God.

Jesus immediately lays His hands on the man, the power of the Spirit flowing through Him, and the man is miraculously raised up.

Here is what is vital for you to remember—and when you comprehend this it will lift the veil from your eyes regarding the role of the Holy Ghost: On earth *Jesus was nothing less than a total man*. He did not have "revelation knowledge" without the voice of the Spirit. And He could not move unless the Holy Spirit moved Him.

Have you ever wondered why, when Jesus passed by, some did not get healed? Why didn't He pray for them? Why didn't He reach out and touch them? It is because the Father did not ask the Holy Ghost to request that Jesus do it. Christ said, "that the world may know that I love the Father, and as the Father gave Me commandment, so I do" (John 14:31). Jesus was dependent on the Spirit; He was Christ's lifeline to the Father.

Was Christ Capable of Sinning?

Even before Christ faced Golgotha, He offered Himself to the Father through the Holy Ghost. Comparing the blood of Christ to the sacrifice of animals, Hebrews says, "How much more shall the blood of Christ, who through the eternal Spirit offered Himself without spot to God, purge your conscience from dead works to serve the living God" (Heb. 9:14).

Had He not offered Himself through the Holy Ghost, He would not be accepted in the eyes of God the Father. Nor would He have endured the sufferings of the cross. Had He not presented Himself through the Holy Ghost, His blood would not have remained pure and spotless.

And let me add this: Had the Holy Spirit not been with Jesus, He may have likely sinned. That's right. It was the Holy Spirit who was the power that kept Him pure. He was not only sent from heaven, but He was called the Son of man—and as such He was capable of sinning. The fact that He *did* not does not mean that He *could* not.

If you believe that Jesus was not able to sin, then why would Satan waste his time tempting Him? The devil knew what he was doing. Without the Holy Ghost Jesus may have never made it.

Jesus actually offered Himself through the Holy Ghost to remain sinless. He even depended on the Spirit to raise Him from the death-grip of the grave. Remember what Paul said? Christ was "declared to be the Son of God with power according to the Spirit of holiness, by the resurrection from the dead" (Rom. 1:4).

It was through the power of the Spirit that Christ was raised from the dead. Here is what Scripture says, "If the Spirit of Him who raised Jesus from the dead dwells in you, He who raised Christ from the dead will also give life to your mortal bodies through His Spirit who dwells in you" (Rom. 8:11). Not only did the Spirit raise Christ; He is the one who will also raise you! We can rest our hope in Him.

God's Master Plan

Even after He changed the course of history by walking out of the empty tomb, Christ continued to depend on the Spirit. In fact, He told the disciples not to leave Jerusalem until they had been endued from on high. He said they should "wait for the Promise of the Father, 'which . . . you have heard from Me; for John truly baptized with water, but you shall be baptized with the Holy Spirit not many days from now' " (Acts 1:4–5).

Christ was under God's control as He spoke those words. He was repeating what the Father said to the Holy Ghost.

So dependent was Christ on the Spirit that He turned to Him before giving directions to His followers. Scripture says He was taken to heaven after He gave instructions "through the Holy Spirit" to the apostles (Acts 1:2).

Don't read me wrong! I am in no way saying that Christ was in a lesser position than the Spirit. Not at all. Jesus is not lower than the Holy Ghost, nor is the Holy Ghost lower than Jesus. There is absolute equality in the Trinity. Each member has unique purposes and characteristics.

What I want you to know is that the Spirit is not weak. He is not immature or incapable of speaking for Himself. The Holy Ghost is perfect, powerful, and glorious.

The Spirit deserves our worship. We should put into practice what we have been singing about for generations: "Praise God from whom all blessings flow. . . . Praise Father, Son, and Holy Ghost."

How do you recognize Him? It's as simple as that little voice you hear when you are about to fall asleep, the voice that reminds you, "You haven't prayed today." Or He may say, "You haven't read the Word today." That's the Spirit speaking, tugging at your soul. You know Him already, but He yearns for you to know Him more.

The Lord predicted what would happen to you when you made a place for the Spirit. He said, "He who believes in Me, as the Scripture has said, out of his heart will flow rivers of living water" (John 7:38). And what was that anointing He was talking about? "But this He spoke concerning the Spirit, whom those believing in Him would receive" (v. 39).

God has a detailed master plan for your life. His anointing and His Spirit are included in the blueprint: "Now He who establishes us with you in Christ and has anointed us is God, who also has sealed us and given us the Spirit in our hearts as a deposit" (2 Cor. 1:21–22).

Have you made room for the Holy Spirit? *All He asks is a place in your heart.*

TEN

"Only a Breath Away"

W hy doesn't God answer my prayer?"

"Why can't I receive my deliverance and my healing?"

The answer to your most urgent need is close—much closer than you ever imagined. Just a word, spoken from your heart, can cause life's darkest clouds suddenly to disappear. It's time to stop thinking that God is an unapproachable Spirit residing millions of miles away. The Father is so near that you can talk to Him at any moment, and His Spirit is so close that He can give you comfort, peace, and direction. All you have to do is ask and trust that He will act.

What I have found in the Spirit is not some mystery-shrouded secret. It is as real as life itself and as close as your very heartbeat. And that's why I want to share it with you.

The Work of the Godhead

"Weakness"? or "Will"?

Let's begin with this fact about the Godhead: What is true of one does not necessarily apply to all three. They are sometimes different, even in the way They move and in the way They talk. We've already discussed the fact that members of the Godhead are distinct persons—yet They are One. But when it comes to our personal relationship and communication with "God," an understanding of Father, Son, and Spirit is essential.

Anytime you see God working, you see Him as one God. But you begin to see some distinction in the way They think and in the way They act.

For example, when the Jewish people under the Old Covenant willfully and knowingly sinned in the presence of the Father, do you recall what happened? Scripture records that they were either slain or punished.

But Christ the Son dealt differently with those who knowingly and willfully sinned. Example: Consider the Pharisees. Did Christ kill them? No! He *rebuked* them.

You say, "Benny, I always believed that Christ forgave everyone." Scripture doesn't record whether Jesus forgave the Pharisees for their sin. Yet He did forgive the criminal on the cross when he cried from his heart, "I'm a sinner!"

Don't misunderstand. God the Father *did* forgive, but he also killed or punished those who refused to stop rebelling against Him. God the Son, however, responded in another manner. Instead of slaying or judging the willful sinner, He simply rebuked him.

You ask, "But what about the Holy Ghost? What is His response to a person who knowingly, deliberately sins?" He reacts differently from even the Father and the Son. The Spirit does not remove them or rebuke them—*He convicts them* and withdraws the power of His presence.

Where Should I Look?

The Trinity, as we see, is comprised of three distinct and unique persons. But you need to understand Their Oneness—Their unity. It is essential that you recognize that the all-embracing Oneness we are talking about is connected to the work and essence of the Godhead.

The Word makes it clear that there are differences—or diversities—of administration in the Godhead, yet They are One. Here is how Paul explained it to the church at Corinth: "There are differences of ministries, but the same Lord. And there are diversities of activities, but it is the same God who works all in all" (1 Cor. 12:5–6). And when he writes, "But the manifestation of the Spirit is given to each one for the profit of all" (v. 7).

Paul was unfolding the working of the Godhead. He explained that the Lord Jesus is the administrator, the Father is the operator, and the Holy Ghost is the manifestor. Now that is one of the few times in the Word where Jesus is mentioned first and the Father second in the order of recognition.

But let's put them back in the "usual" order of Scripture. What is the primary work of the Father? He *operates*. And what about the Son? He *administrates* the operation of the Father. And the Holy Ghost *manifests* the administration of that operation.

If you need life, to whom do you turn? You look to the Father because He is the giver of every good and perfect gift. You say, "Benny, I thought we look to Jesus." No. The source is the Father. But the *giver* of that source is Christ. And the *power* of the source is the Holy Spirit.

So when you need life, here is what happens. You look up to God the Father and say, "Father, give me life!" Or healing. Or deliverance. You see, God is the source of it.

Jesus said, "Ask the Father in My name." Even though you are approaching God through His Son, it is still the Father you are asking for the gift. And your request goes *through* the Son to the Father.

How is that gift returned? Let's say your request is for healing.

God the Father—remember now that God is three persons—looks at God the Son and says, "Would you please heal him?"

Christ delivers the healing. Why? Because that is the role of the administrator. The very word *administrate* means to minister or to serve. So the Father releases the healing to the Son, and the Son serves it to you.

Can you picture yourself reaching out to receive your healing and finding that somehow it seems just out of your reach? You stretch your arms as far as you can, but the gift seems beyond your grasp. So close and yet so far away. What has happened? What's missing?

That's where the work of the Holy Spirit enters the picture. He presents Himself to manifest the healing that was provided by God and served by His Son. *It is the Spirit who completes the process of your healing.*

He's by Your Side

It began at pentecost. The Holy Ghost descended from heaven to make manifest the word of the Godhead. And exactly where is the Spirit today? Where does He make His residence? The Spirit does not stand beside Jesus as many well-intentioned people believe. And He does not stand alongside the Father. He was given to you and to me as *the Comforter* or "the one by our side."

The Holy Spirit is your helper. Yes, He is your assistant to help you receive the life, the healing, or the deliverance you so desperately need.

Often someone asks, "Benny, who should I pray to?"

My answer is, "Please don't confuse the issue. You pray to the Father."

"Well, then," the seeker says, "you told us we are to talk to the Spirit."

I have to tell them, "There is an enormous difference between talking and praying. I've never yet prayed to the Holy Ghost."

Do you know what the meaning of the word *prayer* is? Prayer means "petition." In other words you come with your need asking for an answer. You come looking and expect to receive. You never look to the Spirit—He's the one who *helps* you look.

To this day I have never said, "Holy Spirit, 'give me.'" But I can't count the times I've said, "Precious Holy Spirit, help me ask!"

Are you beginning to realize that your answer is only a breath away? Just a word, waiting to be spoken. It may be a physical problem that has tormented you for years. Or it may be a habit that seems impossible to break. The answer you need is near at hand.

Isn't it time you turn to the Spirit of God and say, "Holy Spirit, You are my helper. I need You. Will You help me now?" The very second you utter those words from your heart, the Holy Ghost will place His hand on you and something marvelous will happen. Suddenly you will find yourself literally "in the Spirit"—absorbed in His presence and His person.

Three Little Words

When the Father gives you something, it comes *of* the Father. And when the Son gives you something, it is usually described as coming *through* Jesus. But when the Holy Ghost provides, it is given *in* Him. *Of, through, in*—just three little words, but they are mighty and powerful.

As you read God's Word, the pattern is striking. When we see the Father spoken of, it is in terms of "the love of God," "the power of God," "the grace of God." That's how God is presented again and again.

But how is Christ portrayed? Often in Scripture we are taught that we "give praise through the Son," "receive through the Son," and so on.

When it comes to the Holy Ghost, however, the terminology changes. The word *in* is used. "Walk in the Spirit, and you shall not fulfill the lust of the flesh" (Gal. 5:16). And "If we live in the Spirit, let us also walk in the Spirit" (v. 25).

As Christ said to the Samaritan woman at the well, "The hour is coming, and now is, when the true worshipers will worship the Father in spirit and truth; for the Father is seeking such to worship Him" (John 4:23). Here, the word *in* simply means "at one with." In other words, Christ said that the Father seeks those that worship and are at one with the Spirit.

Are you walking at one with the Spirit? Are you living at one with the Spirit? Reaching that relationship is not difficult. It is as simple as saying to the Great Helper, "Help me!" That's when the Spirit of God will touch you and actually assist you as you reach out to receive what God wants you to have.

What is important in all of this is that you realize that the Trinity is actually working together to accomplish one goal—to meet your need. They are Father, Son, and Holy Ghost, but They are One. They are a team of persons, united in one nature, working together in complete accord and eternal harmony.

A "Covenant" Relationship

It is because the Holy Ghost is here on earth and by your side that you *keep* the healing or deliverance you have received. That is why Jesus could return to heaven, and yet you can retain on earth the gift He has given. If you want to know how to maintain a close relationship with the Holy Spirit, listen to the word of the great prophet Haggai: "According to the word that I covenanted with you when you came out of Egypt, so My Spirit remains among you; do not fear" (Hag. 2:5).

When you ask the Son of God to come into your heart, you are making a personal covenant with God. And it's not a one-way conversation. God also makes an agreement or a "covenant" with you. That's the way He has always worked.

The Father initiated covenants with Adam, Noah, Abraham, Isaac, David, and many others. But just as God has sought to enter into agreements, so has humanity reached out to God. That is what we discover with Jacob, Joshua, Elijah, and the Israelites.

As the Israelites confessed their sins to God, they said:

> Now therefore, our God,
> The great, the mighty, the awesome God,
> Who keeps covenant and mercy. . . .
> . . . we are in great distress. (Neh. 9:32, 37)

Then Nehemiah told the Lord,

> And because of all this,
> We make a sure covenant, and write it;
> And our leaders and our Levites and our
> priests seal it. (v. 38)

It was signed by no fewer than eighty-four leaders who swore to have "entered into a curse and an oath to walk in God's Law, which was given by Moses the servant of God, and to observe and do all the commandments of the LORD our Lord . . ." (Neh. 10:29).

Covenants with God were ratified by a variety of acts including standing (Ezra 10:14), loosing the shoe (Ruth 4:7–11), giving a feast (Gen. 26:30), erecting a monument (Gen. 31:45–53), and taking an oath (Joshua 2:12–14).

Perhaps the most important covenant of all is the one God made to you through His Son when He "brought up our Lord Jesus from the dead . . . through the blood of the everlasting covenant" (Heb. 13:20).

A Word of Warning

But just as God has a covenant regarding your salvation, you can make a vow or oath with God that deals with your personal needs. I've made a number of commitments to God, and I believe that God recognizes the sincerity of a commitment when you state categorically what you're willing to do in response to His blessing.

One fact is obvious; the Old Testament is filled with covenants that pleased God. And why is that important to you? Because God works by and through covenants, and you can enter into a covenant with Him regarding any special need. You will find that the Father is more than willing to stand by His word.

I have come to believe that the Holy Spirit enters your life as the result of the eternal covenant God made with you regarding our salvation. He is God's messenger—and Christ's—to you from that moment on. And that agreement is to be taken seriously. Remember what happened to Samson. After Delilah had his head shaved while he was sleeping, she shouted, " 'The Philistines are upon you, Samson!' So he awoke from his sleep, and said, 'I will go out as before, at other times, and shake myself free!' But he did not know that the LORD had departed from him" (Judg. 16:20). What had departed was the same "Spirit of the LORD" that "came mightily upon him" earlier (Judg. 15:14).

Can you imagine being in that spot? You think you're filled, but you're not. You believe you're anointed, but the Spirit is gone. Samson was totally unaware that he had betrayed his calling and his covenant with God. He believed he still had strength, but the Spirit had vanished from his life.

The same thing happened to Saul. The Lord rejected Saul as king because "he has turned back from following Me, and has not performed My commandments" (1 Sam. 15:11). Not only did the Spirit leave the king, but something far worse happened: "The Spirit of the LORD departed from Saul, and a distressing spirit from the LORD troubled him" (1 Sam. 16:14).

The Vacuum Will Be Filled

Do you know that every unbeliever is greatly influenced by demons? It sounds shocking, but that's what Scripture says: "And you He made alive, who were dead in trespasses and sins, in which you once walked according to the course of this world, according to the prince of the power of the air, the spirit who now works in the sons of disobedience" (Eph. 2:1–2).

You say, "But that could never happen to me! I'm filled with the Holy Spirit." That may be true, but if for any reason the presence of the Holy Spirit leaves you, a vacuum is created and that is exactly what Satan is looking for. Then his *influence* turns to *oppression*.

Nobody likes to talk about demons. Preachers don't preach about them. Christians don't discuss them. And sinners erase the dreadful topic from their minds. It's like a politician avoiding the subjects of drugs and crime, thinking that somehow they will just go away. But Christ addressed the issue without fear. He talked about how demons are eager to invade your life.

Jesus said to the Pharisees: "When an unclean spirit goes out of a man, he goes through dry places, seeking rest, and finds none. Then he says, 'I will return to my house from which I came.' And when he comes, he finds it empty, swept, and put in order. Then he goes and takes with him seven other spirits more wicked than himself, and they enter and dwell there" (Matt. 12:43–45). Listen closely to what the Lord says next: "And the last state of that man is worse than the first" (v. 45).

Satan's plan of attack is this: Every demon that has left will pay a return visit—to see if the opportunity is still available. And if he is given a chance he will bring others with him. It's a frightening situation, but one that you can avoid by staying completely, totally filled with the Holy Spirit and never breaking your covenant with God.

Do you remember the story of the disciples who failed in their attempt to heal a small child? It was while Christ was on the Mount of Transfiguration being glorified. And when the Master came down from the mountain, the father of the boy said: "Lord, have mercy on my son, for he is an epileptic and suffers severely; for he often falls into the fire and often into the water. So I brought him to Your disciples, but they could not cure him" (Matt. 17:15–16).

But more than a physical healing was needed. Christ said, "'Bring him here to Me.' And Jesus rebuked the demon, and it came out of him; and the child was cured from that very hour" (vv. 17–18).

The Lord not only wants to remove Satan and his demons from your life—those things that are a barrier to your healing and deliverance—but He wants to fill that empty void. That's why He sent the Comforter. He wants you to be *filled* with the Spirit.

Right now, the Spirit is on earth. In fact He is waiting patiently for your invitation.

All it takes is just a word, even a whisper—"Holy Spirit, please help me!"

Your answer is only a breath away.

ELEVEN

"Why Are You Weeping?"

"Benny, can blasphemy against the Father be forgiven?" a new Christian asked recently.

"Yes," I answered.

"What about blasphemy against the Son?"

"That can be forgiven too," I said.

"Then can you tell me why blasphemy against the Holy Ghost can't be forgiven?"

Freedom from Fear

For many people the topic is troublesome. But the Spirit has given me freedom from the fear of committing "the unpardonable sin." He unlocked my understanding with such a revelation that I no longer worry over the subject.

"He Was Quietly Weeping"

In the winter of 1974 God opened my eyes to a tremendous truth regarding the nature of the Holy Spirit and why the Father and the Son gave the "ultimate" warning to those who would blaspheme the Spirit.

I was in prayer when suddenly I knew that the Spirit of God was in my room, and I felt He was weeping. I know it sounds strange, and I must confess I don't fully understand it. But I do remember that I was on my knees when I felt His presence and sensed that He was quietly weeping.

You say, "Well, how did you know it was the Spirit?" For me to question the reality of that moment would be to question my salvation; that's how real that experience was. I can't explain it or comprehend it, but I know it happened.

The experience was so real that I literally turned my face to the left and said, "Spirit of the Lord, why are You weeping?"

There was no answer. And at that moment the tears began flowing down my own cheeks. Through my watering eyes I asked Him again, "Spirit of the Lord, why are You weeping?"

Then suddenly my entire being began to cry out. It was no longer just tears; the reality of what I felt was so great I began to groan. The feeling came from deep inside. It was as if I were heartbroken—like a person who has just lost a son or a daughter.

The deep sobbing would not stop. I was weeping at night and could not sleep. And it continued, not for hours but for days. It wasn't planned, and, truthfully, I couldn't understand why the tears were so uncontrollable. In all, the experience lasted for more than three weeks.

The burden became heavier and heavier. I felt as if someone had taken a thousand-pound load, strapped it on my back, pulled tight its belts, locked it with a key, and left me alone to struggle. If anything, it felt as if I was overburdened with an oppressive, heavy load of grief. That's the only way to describe it—a weight of grief.

Pacing the Floor

I felt like the psalmist when he wrote,

> I am weary with my groaning;
> All night I make my bed swim;
> I drench my couch with my tears. (Ps. 6:6)

There I was, grieving and not knowing why, pacing the floor and searching for a reason.

I looked up and said, "Lord, why?" I prayed to be released from this unexplainable weight on my shoulders. At that moment God Almighty transformed that heaviness of grief into a burden for lost souls that I had never known before.

What began with my turning to ask the Holy Spirit, "Why are you weeping?" ended with a life-changing burden for the lost that has never left me—not once—to this day.

I came away from that experience (even though I still do not understand it fully) convinced that the Holy Spirit grieves for the world. I am fully persuaded that with tears He searches for servants to spread God's love. I believe that the Spirit of the Father's heart is breaking with the needs of mankind. Perhaps for those weeks He allowed me just a glimpse of His agony for the lost.

There was no question of what was to be the future of Benny Hinn. I knew that I *must* preach the message of the Father, the Son, and the Holy Spirit. And I have not stopped doing it since.

The Spirit is so special that when He finds a person that He can use, He allows them to feel His heartbeat. When you have felt the pain that the Holy Ghost feels, it clings to your consciousness and will never leave you. You not only see the needs of mankind; you *feel* those desperate needs as never before.

But I believe there was another reason that God allowed me to endure that lesson. It opened my eyes to why the Holy Spirit is a member of the Trinity and yet is different from the Father and the Son. And it made it possible for me to fit together the pieces of the puzzle called "the unpardonable sin."

Insult and Slander

Exactly what does Scripture say?

Jesus, speaking to the Pharisees, said, "He who is not with Me is against Me, and he who does not gather with Me scatters abroad. Therefore I say to you, every sin and blasphemy will be forgiven men, but the blasphemy against the Spirit will not be forgiven men" (Matt. 12:30–31). Then, making it even clearer, He said: "Anyone who speaks a word against the Son of Man, it will be forgiven him; but whoever speaks against the Holy Spirit, it will not be forgiven him, either in this age or in the age to come" (v. 32).

What does the word *blasphemy* encompass? The word has several meanings including

To speak evil of
To rail (or scoff)
To revile—or to abuse, reproach, or speak profanity of
To defame—to speak with injury
To slander—or to accuse falsely
To insult

Some may ask, "How do you defame the Holy Ghost?" Or "How do you insult Him?" It is a *willful* act.

The book of Hebrews speaks directly to the issue:

If we sin willfully after we have received the knowledge of the truth, there no longer remains a sacrifice for sins, but a certain fearful expectation of judgment, and fiery indignation which will devour the adversaries. Anyone who has rejected Moses' law dies without mercy on the testimony of two or three witnesses. Of how much worse punishment, do you suppose, will he be thought worthy who has trampled the Son of God underfoot, counted the blood of the covenant by which he was sanctified a common thing, and insulted the Spirit of grace? (Heb. 10:26–29)

The words are followed by this stern reminder: "For we know Him who said, 'Vengeance is Mine; I will repay,' says the Lord. And again, 'The LORD will judge His people.' It is a fearful thing to fall into the hands of the living God" (vv. 30–31).

What a Difference

Why is there no forgiveness for blasphemy against the Holy Spirit? Throughout the pages of this book I have shared with you from Scripture that there is a uniqueness—a *difference*—in the Holy Ghost. He is not higher nor lower than the Father or the Son, but we must come to know His characteristics.

God Almighty, the Father, is the great God of heaven and must be worshiped, praised, glorified, magnified, and uplifted. Jesus, His Son, is the Lord of glory, whom even the angels fear to look upon. I feel also that the Holy Spirit has the capacity to feel human emotions—even pain, grief, and anguish—with an intensity that is known uniquely to Him.

You say, "Do you mean that the Holy Ghost can feel heartache in a different way than the Father and the Son?" Scripture does not say, "Grieve not the Father or the Son." It is always, "Grieve not the Spirit." Why? I believe it is because He is touched in a deep, profound way that somehow varies from what the other members of the Godhead experience.

The very fact that Jesus said that "a word against the Son of Man will be forgiven" but "a word against the Holy Spirit will not be forgiven" indicates that the Holy Ghost can become wounded.

Why is it that the Father would say, "You have vexed my Spirit"? In other words, God's Spirit was afflicted or tormented. And Scripture records that "He turned Himself against them as an enemy, and He fought against them" (Isa. 63:10). Why is it that the Holy Ghost seems to be so protected? Perhaps it is because God the Father knows how tender the Spirit is. It is almost as though God the Father were saying, "If you touch Him, I'll never forgive you."

Why is the Holy Ghost so shielded by Christ that Jesus would say, "My blood will wash every sin but that"? He even said, "But he who blasphemes against the Holy Spirit never has forgiveness, but is subject to eternal condemnation" (Mark 3:29). Why? Again it is because the Holy Spirit is different and His heart can so easily be touched with pain.

But may I give you a word of comfort? Before Jesus ever talked about blasphemy, He made a very important statement you should read once again. He said: "He who is not with Me is against Me, and he who does not gather with Me scatters abroad" (Matt. 12:30).

If you are working for Christ, you do not fall into the category of His warning. When the Lord spoke on the topic of blasphemy, He made it absolutely clear that He was admonishing people who were not working with Him.

Ask yourself, "Am I with Him?" If the answer is yes, then ask, "Do I gather souls for Him?" If the answer is still yes, you can say, "Then I will never blaspheme the Spirit."

"Are You Worried?"

A teenage girl once came to me convinced she had blasphemed the Holy Ghost.

"Are you worried?" I asked her.

"Yes," she said with a troubled look.

"Young lady," I said, "the very fact that you are worried means that you did not blaspheme the Spirit."

You see, blasphemy is an act of the will that does not carry worry with it.

Blasphemy is cursing Jesus and saying, "I don't care what He did!" It is saying, "Who cares how precious the blood is?" Blasphemy is insulting what God did and doing it willfully.

You say, "Well, Benny, how do I know I'll never commit that sin?" You will not commit that sin as long as you never *want* to commit it.

Look closely at what Christ said. He said anyone who "speaks" against the Spirit will not be forgiven. That word is vital to Christ's message. To speak indicates a deliberate act. It's more than an idle thought. Your entire body becomes involved in the act of uttering a word.

If the Spirit is blasphemed, He is reviled by those who have made a *decision* to blaspheme. It's an act of volition, a choice you must exercise.

Where is Satan in all of this? From dealing with people as a minister I know how the devil comes to people and tries to fill their minds with evil thoughts about the Holy Ghost. Would you expect any less of them? Perhaps it has happened to you.

Have you ever had some "unbecoming" thought enter your mind that you wish had never come? Who launched that evil thought in your direction? Of course it was Satan. But did you speak that thought out loud? No! The reason you kept silent was that it was not your thought.

It is the person who speaks against the Holy Ghost who has made a decision to blaspheme. It is the one who says, "I'm going to blaspheme, and I don't care what God thinks!"

Saul blasphemed the Holy Ghost when he rejected the word of God. Demas, one of Paul's companions, blasphemed when he turned his back on the gospel and returned to the lusts of the flesh. Paul wrote, "Demas has forsaken me, having loved this present world, and has departed for Thessalonica" (2 Tim. 4:10).

Don't Let Him Leave

You say, "You have been telling us that we can't blaspheme. What about Saul and Demas?" The point I am making is that you can't blaspheme as long as you decide to live for Jesus and stick with it.

The road to eternity is littered with people who start out with Christ and end up with Satan. There are those who walk an aisle and shake a preacher's hand as some kind of an insurance policy on a mansion in heaven. But their hearts did not follow their actions. Soon you find those same people falling in love with lust or money or the glitter of the world. And they say, "God, I'm leaving."

You may wonder, "How do I know that the Holy Spirit is still with me? And how will I know when and if He has departed?"

It is a device of Satan to attack you and fill your mind with the words, "The Holy Spirit has left you. He's gone forever. You'll never have Him back!"

But don't accept that. Here's how you can know that the Spirit is still with you. This has been a great help to me and I believe it will be to you. First, the Scriptures tell us the Holy Spirit abides with every believer as counselor and source of peace. Second, *are you aware of the presence of Jesus in your life?* Then the Holy Ghost has not left. *Do you still hear the Spirit of God say, "Pray!"* He hasn't left. *Do you sometimes feel guilty about not reading the Word?* He has not departed; in fact, He's convicting you. *Have you met someone and felt the urge to tell the person about Jesus?* He's still there.

Jesus was not speaking a contradiction when He said the Spirit will be with you forever. He was speaking of the fact that the Spirit's role is permanent—even eternal. You see, if you blaspheme Him, the Spirit will depart. But if you grieve Him, He doesn't leave you. He'll stay, even when you wound Him. I believe Christians grieve the Spirit every day. I, for one, am guilty.

Grieving the Holy Ghost is the sin of the church. That's why Paul said to the church, "Do not grieve the Spirit." He was not addressing those words to unbelievers.

What If I Should Fail?

You may ask, "How do we grieve Him?" You grieve Him when you don't forgive. You grieve Him when you say something ugly or wrong. But your daily prayer should be: "Blessed Spirit of God, please help me today not to grieve You."

And what if you should fail? He is more than willing to hear you say, "Please forgive me." And He will forgive and cleanse you seventy times seven.

The Holy Spirit is so gentle that even the slightest wound will cause Him pain. And the longer you've known Him, the more you will understand His feelings. So many times, in tears, I say, "Holy Spirit, I'm sorry for the anguish I've caused you. But please, please, stay by my side."

There are times I've told Him: "You can chastise me, but don't let me go!" For whom the Lord chastises He loves. It's like saying, "I love you."

I believe that if a person remains in a state of unforgiveness the Spirit of the Lord will allow tormentors to enter him. That's what Christ told Peter when the disciple asked, "Lord, how often shall my brother sin against me, and I forgive him? Up to seven times?" (Matt. 18:21).

The Lord answered, "I do not say to you, up to seven times, but up to seventy times seven" (v. 22). Then He gave the parable of the unforgiving servant, which ends with the warning, " 'Should you not also have had compassion on your fellow servant, just as I had pity on you?' And his master was angry, and delivered him to the torturers until he should pay all that was due to him" (vv. 33–34).

Christ concluded the parable by saying, "So My heavenly Father will do to you if each of you, from his heart, does not forgive his brother" (v. 35).

Does this mean that the Holy Ghost has made a permanent retreat? No. It's just that God will remove His hand of protection from those who won't forgive.

A person who has totally blasphemed the Holy Spirit becomes filled with the demons of Satan. But if you ask, "Benny, do you believe that a demon can possess a Christian who is filled with the Holy Ghost?" Absolutely not!

I do believe, however, that a person who has made a confession of faith in Christ, but is not living for the Lord—who is living in unforgiveness—can be influenced by demons. They can be harassed and even *oppressed* by the powers of darkness, but not possessed.

Peter, for example, said, "Lord, you're not going to die." And Jesus said, "Get behind me, Satan." Peter was not possessed by Satan. He was influenced. There is a big difference.

Jesus said, through the Spirit, "I will never leave you nor forsake you." And that, my friend, is good news. And since He is staying, it is more important to know what He will do for us than what Satan will do against us.

You Can't Do It Alone

I am certain that it is your utmost desire to love God with your spirit, soul, and body. But no matter how strong your desire, it is absolutely impossible to accomplish your goal all alone. It is imperative that you say, "Holy Spirit, I'm asking you to assist me."

Paul wrote to the church at Rome, "Now hope does not disappoint, because the love of God has been poured out in our hearts by the Holy Spirit who was given to us" (Rom. 5:5).

Certainly we want to love Christ, but it is impossible unless the Spirit gives us supernatural love. And how do you receive it? You simply say, "Spirit of God, I surrender to you." By that very act He will flood your soul with a love for the Lord.

The more deeply you know the Holy Spirit, the more deeply you will know Jesus. It's automatic. Why? Because when the Spirit is present, Christ is promoted. Jesus said, "He shall glorify Me!" The Lord is never pushed aside, but rather He is pulled much closer.

Paul wrote, "There is therefore now no condemnation to those who are in Christ Jesus, who do not walk according to the flesh, but according to the Spirit" (Rom. 8:1).

Do you understand what it truly means to walk after the Spirit? When He says, "Pray," that's what you'll do. When He says, "Testify," that's what you'll do. Suddenly, you're walking after the Spirit.

The Joy of Freedom in the Spirit

To disobey is to feel condemnation and then guilt. But if you heed His call, you know the joy of freedom in the Spirit: "For the law of the Spirit of life in Christ Jesus has made me free from the law of sin and death" (Rom. 8:2). The lawgiver in the Old Covenant was the Father, but the lawgiver in the New Covenant is the Holy Ghost. Jesus gave the commandments *through* the Spirit (Acts 1:2), just as God once gave the law *through* Moses.

Seven Revelations

What a joy to dwell on the victories described by Paul in Romans 8. In fact Paul shares seven specific revelations in the first sixteen verses of his letter.

Perhaps nowhere in Scripture is the work of the Spirit so clearly defined.

1. *There is power over sin.* The first revelation says that the law of the Spirit of life gives you freedom from sin and death (vv. 1–2). You'll have dominion over sin.

2. *He will fulfill the law.* "For what the law could not do in that it was weak through the flesh, God did by sending His own Son in the likeness of sinful flesh . . . that the righteous requirement of the law might be fulfilled in us who do not walk according to the flesh but according to the Spirit" (vv. 3–4).

It is the fulfillment of the Law of Moses that has produced the freedom we now have in the Spirit.

3. *He will give you the mind of God.* "Those who love according to the flesh set their minds on the things of the flesh, but those who live according to the Spirit, the things of the Spirit. For to be carnally minded is death, but to be spiritually minded is life and peace. Because the carnal mind is enmity against God; for it is not subject to the law of God, nor indeed can be. So then, those who are in the flesh cannot please God" (vv. 5–8).

4. *He will give you righteousness.* "But you are not in the flesh but in the Spirit, if indeed the Spirit of God dwells in you. Now if anyone does not have the Spirit of Christ, he is not His. And if Christ is in you, the body is dead because of sin, but the Spirit is life because of righteousness" (vv. 9–10).

5. *He will give life to your body.* "But if the Spirit of Him who raised Jesus from the dead dwells in you, He who raised Christ from the dead will also give life to your mortal bodies through His Spirit who dwells in you" (v. 11).

If you follow in the footsteps of the Holy Ghost, you will walk in health. You will have a quickened body. As the prophet Isaiah said, "Those who wait on the LORD shall renew their strength" (40:31). My friend, you cannot renew your strength without the Holy Ghost because He is the one who quickens the mortal body.

6. *He will bring death to self.* "Therefore, brethren, we are debtors—not to the flesh, to live according to the flesh. For if you live according to the flesh you will die; but if by the Spirit you put to death the deeds of the body, you will live. For as many as are led by the Spirit of God, these are sons of God" (vv. 12–14).

7. *He will testify of your salvation.* "For you did not receive the spirit of bondage again to fear, but you received the Spirit of adoption by whom we cry out, 'Abba, Father.' The Spirit Himself bears witness with our spirit that we are children of God" (vv. 15–16).

In verse after verse Paul tells you that it is the Spirit that does the work of the Father and the Son. And I get excited every time I read those glorious words: "For as many as are led by the Spirit of God, these are sons of God."

God does not intend for you to stray from the path He has set for you to follow. He did not create you to see you fail. That's why you should not become unduly alarmed by the possibility of committing the unpardonable sin, blasphemy against the Holy Spirit.

Your love for Christ so outweighs Satan's influence that the battle has already been won. The Holy Spirit is longing for you to begin a deep, personal relationship.

When my soul cried out with a heartfelt sobbing that seemed unending, the Spirit was patiently waiting. His burden became my burden, and the experience gave me a passion for souls that has never diminished nor departed.

He was waiting to give me power, fulfillment, righteousness, a Spirit-led life, and so much more.

And now He is waiting for you.

TWELVE

Heaven on Earth

M y first "sermons" in 1974 and early 1975 did not have much content. They were basically my testimony of the work of the Spirit—of how He made Himself so real to me. In those days I really didn't know too much, and there was so much to learn.

Following the Spirit's Voice

But during 1975 I heard the unmistakable voice of the Holy Spirit telling me that it was time to begin conducting weekly meetings in Toronto. He said, "Follow me. Hear My voice, and you will lead many to Christ."

And so I began. On Monday nights we scheduled a series of services that would continue for the next five years. We started in a high school auditorium, and the crowds became so large we had to move to larger facilities. Hundreds and hundreds of people attended.

The services were totally led by the Spirit, and I listened ever so closely to His voice. People were delivered from serious addictions.

Families were reunited. We had "healing lines" and heard testimonies of miracles. But always, always, the services resulted in the salvation of lost souls.

Then something happened. People began to receive miracles, deliverance, and healings right in their seats. No lines for "the laying on of hands." God began to do His work all across the auditorium—so freely that there was not time to hear all of the testimonies.

The press began to take notice. On the front pages of the *Toronto Star*, the *Toronto Globe and Mail*, and other papers across Canada there were stories of the "Miracle Rallies" we were conducting.

In December 1976 the *Globe and Mail* sent a reporter to one of the services to describe in detail what was happening. He wrote of the healings and testimonies and ended the article by quoting me: "I'm not interested in building up Benny Hinn. I'm not and never will be. Jesus is the one . . . to be built up and exalted. We want to reach souls for the Lord Jesus. I want to see souls, souls, souls, souls, souls. People, do you understand that?"

Under the headline, "Does Faith Healing Really Work?" the *Toronto Star* presented four case studies of people who had been healed in our services. He told about a shift worker at the GM plant in Oshawa who had cancer of the throat. "This week, following a checkup at the cancer clinic, he was told there is no trace of malignancy."

He told the story of a Beavertown trucker: "A nonchurchgoer, who had suffered from congestive heart failure and slight emphysema (a lung disease) for seven years, was persuaded by friends to attend a healing crusade. 'I went to the doctor three days later, and he told me he could find nothing wrong,' he says. 'God must have done it.'"

What about their doctors? The reporter quoted one as saying,

"Look, there are more things happening in this world than we know about."

Television stations began to film documentaries on what God was doing. The Canadian Broadcasting Corporation (CBC), Global RV, and the huge independent station in Toronto, Channel 9, produced specials. We ran our own weekly television program that was shown in prime time after *60 Minutes* for a year and a half.

A Yellow Cab in Pittsburgh

Leaving the great city of Toronto in 1979 was not easy for me. It was where I had been saved, healed, and touched by the mighty Spirit of God. The press had nothing but good news to report about the ministry. But again, I promised to follow the leading of the Holy Ghost.

I knew He wanted me to build a church and establish an international ministry. He had told me this years earlier, in 1977. I remember exactly where it happened. I was back in Pittsburgh, riding in a big Yellow Cab when I had a conversation with the Spirit about it. About the ministry He said, "It will touch the world!"

I wondered, "Where will it be? New York? Los Angeles?" But you know, the Spirit has an amazing way of leading you.

In July 1978 I traveled to Orlando, Florida, to speak for Pastor Roy Harthern. He told me about his daughter, Suzanne, who was attending Evangel College in Springfield, Missouri. Being single, my ears perked up.

I invited myself back to spend Christmas with them, and Suzanne was home for the holidays. The first time I saw her, the Lord said, "That's your wife." Just like that! I felt it. And she did too.

But I had to be sure so I began to ask God for "signs." I'd put out "fleeces." And every one of them was answered. I thought, *Is this just coincidence? Or does God really want me to marry this young lady?*

Then I tried one last sign—a rather difficult one.

I was flying back to Orlando from San Jose, California, on January 1, 1979. I made a quick trip there to speak at a New Year's Eve service. On the plane I had a talk with God. I said, "If she really is to be my wife, have her say to me when I get back, 'I've made you a cheesecake.'" That was the toughest test I could think of.

Suzanne met me at the Orlando airport, and the first words out of her mouth were, "Benny, I've made you a cheesecake." Then she said, "Don't expect too much. I've never made a cheesecake before."

We were engaged within two weeks and married later that year.

As time passed, all signs pointed to Orlando, Florida, as the place we would begin a worldwide ministry. With just a handful of people, the Orlando Christian Center was started in 1983. Now it touches the lives of thousands of people every week, plus a national television audience.

He's Not a Promoter

To be honest, I had no idea where the Spirit would lead my life when I began my relationship with Him. All I knew was that He was real and desired my fellowship. He wanted to be my teacher and guide.

But here is what I have come to know. The Holy Ghost will never promote Himself; He'll promote Jesus. He will never create the place of greatness just for Himself; He'll give the honor to the Lord.

I've also learned that the Spirit is not the source of God's gifts. He is the one who helps you *receive* from the giver, who is God the Father. He's also the one who helps you *receive* God the Son as Savior and Lord.

Your Claim on the Spirit

Even an unbeliever senses the power of the Holy Ghost! I've talked to hundreds of people about their conversion experiences, and so many have told me, "Something was happening that I couldn't explain. I felt uncomfortable about things I was doing." That's the convicting power of the Spirit.

The Lord said, "My Spirit shall not strive with man forever" (Gen. 6:3). There is a "wrestling" going on as the Holy Ghost tries to let you know that you need the Lord. That's why people are so uncomfortable in the presence of God before they are saved.

The Spirit is actually a witness for Jesus! "When the Helper comes, whom I shall send to you from the Father, the Spirit of truth who proceeds from the Father, He will testify of Me" (John 15:26). The Spirit's vital purpose is to lead people to Christ.

The Spirit convicts and convinces. I've met people who have left a gospel meeting and felt literally "hounded" by the Holy Spirit. They felt miserable in their sin. They felt a continual tugging at their hearts. The Spirit wouldn't let them go until they had made their peace with God through His Son.

He will enter your mind and present the truth of Scripture, convincing you of the validity of the gospel.

And after you have given your heart to Christ, He is still right there, helping you witness for the Lord. The prophet Micah wrote:

> But truly I am full of power by the Spirit of the LORD,
> And of justice and might,
> To declare to Jacob his transgression
> And to Israel his sin. (Mic. 3:8)

He gives you the power to speak. In fact, it's useless to attempt to proclaim God's Word without the Holy Ghost upon you.

"Help Me!"

When you say, "Holy Spirit, help me to know Jesus," He will not disappoint you. He is always willing to help. Listen to what the psalmist says: "Do not cast me away from Your presence, and do not take Your Holy Spirit from me" (Ps. 51:11). Then, in the very next breath, he says, "Restore to me the joy of Your salvation; and uphold me with Your generous Spirit" (v. 12). The Holy Ghost is willing.

Anytime you say, "Help me," He says, "I will."

When you say, "Teach me," He says, "I'm ready."

And when you say, "Help me to pray," He says, "Let's begin."

He is right there, giving you the *desire* to pray. He is the urging behind the hunger to talk to the Father and to the Son. Paul wrote these powerful words: "Therefore I make known to you that no one speaking by the Spirit of God calls Jesus accursed, and no one can say that Jesus is Lord except by the Holy Spirit" (1 Cor. 12:3). When you sing "He is Lord" and mean it from your heart, it's proof that the Holy Ghost is within you. He's using you to proclaim that Jesus Christ is Lord to the whole world!

The moment you confess the death, burial, and resurrection of Christ you have passed the test of the Spirit. Scripture says, "By this you know the Spirit of God: Every spirit that confesses that Jesus Christ has come in the flesh is of God, and every spirit that does not confess that Jesus Christ has come in the flesh is not from God" (1 John 4:2–3). He says, "By this we know the spirit of truth and the spirit of error" (v. 6).

Your salvation is at the very heart of the work of the Holy Spirit. In fact, it is He that actually adopts you into God's family. Paul writes, "For as many as are led by the Spirit of God, these are sons of God. For you did not receive the spirit of bondage again to fear, but you received the Spirit of adoption" (Rom. 8:14–15).

And here is how you express it. By Him "we cry out, 'Abba, Father.' The Spirit Himself bears witness with our spirit that we are children of God, and if children, then heirs—heirs of God and joint heirs with Christ, if indeed we suffer with Him, that we may also be glorified together" (vv. 15–17).

Up for Adoption

The Spirit looked at you and saw an orphan. He said, "I will adopt you." He's your Father. Why? Because He is the Spirit of the Father. Do you remember Dottie Rambo's song, "Holy Spirit, You Are Welcome in This Place"? She was inspired to write, "Omnipotent Father of mercy and grace." That's what the Spirit is.

Without Him it is impossible to approach the Father. Paul tells you, "For through Him we both have access by one Spirit to the Father" (Eph. 2:18). Through whom? Through Jesus, both Jew and Gentile can approach God by the Holy Ghost.

But here's the most exciting part of all. *The Bible says that the Holy Ghost has been given to you as a guarantee of eternal life.* "Having believed, you were sealed with the Holy Spirit of promise, who is the guarantee of our inheritance until the redemption of the purchased possession, to the praise of His glory" (Eph. 1:13–14).

There's no doubt about it. The Holy Spirit is preparing you for heaven. If you're convinced He's living inside, then you must never question whether you are born again. You must never question whether your home is heaven. And you must never question whether you will have eternal life.

Let me put it this way. If tomorrow morning you walk into a store and pick out some clothes and a pair of shoes but don't have all the money, you walk over to "layaway" and make a down payment toward the purchase. You say, "I'll pick it up next week." Your name is on the bill, and you take the receipt home. Then next week you pick up the purchased possession.

That's exactly what Jesus did when He came and gave you the Holy Ghost. The only difference is that He paid the entire price on Calvary. But here's what He says: "I paid for your life, but I'm also giving a down payment that guarantees it's mine." He sent the Holy Spirit. And if you have Him, you are on your way to glory.

When Christ returns, He's going to pick you up and take you home. It's worth shouting about. You are a purchased possession of the Lord. That's why you can tell Satan to his ugly face, "Don't touch me. I'm a possession of Christ!" And don't be afraid to speak the Word. Kick him out, and he will flee from you.

You have the Holy Spirit. A "deposit" on your inheritance! Why was He given as a down payment? Paul says, "Christ has redeemed us from the curse of the law, having become a curse for us (for it is written, 'Cursed is everyone who hangs on a tree')" (Gal. 3:13). And then he wrote this marvelous truth: He redeemed us in order "that the blessing of Abraham might come upon the Gentiles in Christ Jesus, that we might receive the promise of the Spirit through faith" (v. 14).

Because Christ became a curse, the Spirit was given as promised.

You Need Some Help

From the moment you accept Jesus as Savior, it is the Spirit that gives you the will, the strength, and the desire to obey God and live the Christian life. Without Him it is impossible.

The apostle Peter tells you, "Since you have purified your souls in obeying the truth through the Spirit in sincere love of the brethren, love one another fervently with a pure heart" (1 Peter 1:22).

The reason people—even Christians—fail is that they depend

on their own strength. You can't obey God by saying, "I'm going to do it by myself." How many times have you said, "I'm going to pray," but you didn't. Or "I'll read the Word," but you forgot. Why? Because you were depending on your mind. You depended on the flesh, and it will fail you continually.

He'll give you strength and life, but the Spirit will give you something else just as important. *He'll give you rest.* Isaiah said,

> As a beast goes down into the valley,
> And the Spirit of the LORD causes him to rest,
> So You lead Your people,
> To make Yourself a glorious name. (Isa. 63:14)

Just after I began to preach the gospel, I met David DuPlessis. He was known as "Mr. Pentecost" as a result of his presentations of the Holy Spirit to world religious leaders. He was a charismatic before anyone knew what the word meant.

I was walking down the same hallway with this anointed man at a conference in Brockville, Ontario, when I summoned the courage to stop him and ask a question. I nervously asked him. "Dr. DuPlessis, how can I truly please God?"

The old man, who is now with Jesus, stopped, put his briefcase down, pointed his finger in my chest and pushed me against the wall. I certainly didn't expect that from a frail preacher. All I had said was, "How can I please God?" and he nailed me to the wall. Then he said two words that I have never forgotten. He said: "Don't try!" He picked up his little case and walked on down the hall.

I caught up with him and said, "Dr. DuPlessis, I don't understand."

He calmly turned around and said, "Young man, it's not *your* ability. *It's His ability in you.*" Then he said, "Good night," and walked into his room.

As I walked into my room, I was still puzzled. I lay down on my bed and thought about those words. "It's not *your* ability. *It's His ability in you.*"

In that moment I hardly knew what to pray, but the Spirit began to unlock the truth of those words to me. How can I please God? By yielding! By not even trying. It was just as Mr. Pentecost said. The Holy Spirit will do the work. It's not my strength; it's His. Otherwise I would boast of my own accomplishments.

God's Touch

When you see Jesus face to face, you won't say, "Lord, look what I did." You'll say, "Lord, look what you did with this wretched man." Start practicing it. Open your arms wide and say, "Spirit of the living God, I want to live for Jesus today. I give You my mind, my emotion, my will, my intellect, my lips, my mouth, my ears, and my eyes—use them for the glory of God."

When I wake up and pray that kind of prayer, the anointing floods me like an ocean at high tide. In the moment I totally surrender, God begins to flow through my ministry. Nothing less will do.

I have often wondered why, in my own meetings, the Spirit directs me so often to pray for healing. And I have wondered why my ministry has been accompanied by people who fall under the power of the Holy Spirit. But when I look at the results of the meetings, I see that every manifestation of the Spirit is for one purpose: to bring people to Christ.

It is a demonstration that God is alive, that He is still "moving" in the lives of people. I have seen thousands of people literally fall under the power of the Spirit, and I believe that just a small touch of God's power is all they felt. But it demonstrates the awesome strength of the Almighty, and it draws people to the Savior.

Being healed or even being "slain in the Spirit" is not a pre-requisite for heaven. There is only one door—Christ the Lord. Never take your attention from the purpose of the Spirit on earth. He is the Spirit of the Father and the Spirit of the Son, leading people to confess that Christ is Lord.

As I began my ministry I never ceased to be amazed at the power of the Holy Spirit. He's gentle, but He's powerful.

> The grass withers, the flower fades,
> Because the breath of the LORD blows upon it.
> Surely the people are grass. (Isa. 40:7)

The Holy Ghost is not a weak personality.

As both a young Christian and a new minister I often stood back and watched the Lord at work. I knew it wasn't me that was touching lives. It was the sovereignty of God and the operation of the Spirit. I just watched in amazement.

But I don't think I've been as frightened in my life as that Sunday night on April 1975. There I was on the platform of a small pentecostal church on the west side of Toronto when my parents—Costandi and Clemence—walked in the door.

My heart almost stopped, and I could feel the perspiration on my forehead. My worst nightmare could not have matched this. I was petrified—too startled to laugh and too shocked to cry.

What Must They Be Thinking?

I had been preaching for five months, but my parents had no idea. The tension in our house over the Lord was bad enough without my breaking that news. But they saw an ad the pastor placed in the newspaper and walked into that little church.

I couldn't even glance in their direction. But the moment I

opened my mouth to preach, the anointing of the Holy Spirit filled that building. It was so strong. Words began flowing out of me like a river. I found myself actually "listening" to what the Spirit directed me to say.

As I was finishing my message, I felt led to begin ministering to people who needed healing. I thought, *What must my mom and dad be thinking of all this?* Then they stood up and walked out the back door.

"Jim," I said after the service, "you've got to pray!" Jim Poynter was with me on the platform that night and knew the seriousness of the situation. I even thought of spending the night at his home to avoid the inevitable confrontation.

Instead, I got into my car and began to drive the streets of Toronto. I thought, "If I get home in the middle of the night, my folks will be sleeping." It was just after two o'clock in the morning when I quietly parked in front of the house and turned off the ignition.

I tiptoed up the steps and slowly unlocked the front door. I opened it and was startled by what I saw. There in front of me, seated on the couch, were my mom and dad.

I had been panic-stricken when I saw them walk into that church, but this was even worse. My knees began to tremble, and I looked for a place to sit down.

My father was the first to speak and I listened in disbelief.

"Son," he softly said, "how can we become like you?"

Was I hearing what I thought I was hearing? Was this the same man that had been so offended by my conversion? The father that had absolutely forbidden the name of "Jesus" to be spoken in our home?

"We really want to know," he said. "Tell us how we can have what you have."

I looked at my dear mother and saw tears begin to fall down her beautiful cheeks. I couldn't contain my joy at that moment. I began to weep. And for the next hour of that unforgettable night I opened the Scripture and led my parents to the saving knowledge of the Lord Jesus Christ.

My daddy said, "Benny, do you know what convinced me?" He told me that when I began preaching, he turned to my mother and said, "That's not your son. Your son can't talk! His God must be real." He didn't know that I had been totally healed of stuttering.

The marvelous conversion of my parents allowed the Lord to literally sweep through the rest of the family. Henry showed up and got saved. My little brother Mike was born again. Then it happened to Chris. If you've ever heard about "household salvation," this was it!

The Hinn home was transformed into "heaven on earth!" And the change was not temporary. It was a *permanent* work of the Spirit. Today Chris, Willie, Henry, Sammy, and Mike are totally involved in ministry. Mary and Rose are committed Christians and living for the Lord. And Benny? Well, you know what has happened to him.

First Things First

Just as the Holy Spirit touched my life and drew my parents to Christ, He wants the same for you. The greatest work of the Spirit is not to lead you into some heavenly ecstasy on earth. That may happen, but His purpose is to convict of sin and lead people to Jesus.

As you have been reading this book you may have said, "That's for me! I want to have an exciting personal relationship with the Holy Spirit!" But are you ready for it? What happened to me the night the Spirit entered my bedroom was not the first step. It began much earlier. You've got to put first things first and touch every step on your spiritual ladder.

My friend, if you have never asked Christ to come into your heart, now is the time. It's the most important step you will ever take. Right now, say: "Jesus, I confess that I am a sinner. I believe that You are the Son of God and that You shed your precious blood on the cross for me. Forgive me of my sin. Cleanse my heart from all unrighteousness. I thank You for saving me now. Amen."

If you have spoken that prayer from your heart, you are ready to begin a new life in the Spirit. And every day as you pray, read God's Word, and tell others of His love, you will sense God's exciting direction.

I have come to the conclusion that I am totally dependent on the Holy Spirit. He's all I have. He's all you have. Jesus promised Him and God sent Him that you may have knowledge, power, communion, and fellowship. He will anoint you, help you, breathe on you, comfort you, give you rest, lead and guide you, help you pray, and so much more.

He is waiting to begin a relationship with you that will change your life forever. But it's up to you to extend the invitation.

When the sun comes up tomorrow, He will be longing to hear you say, "Good morning, Holy Spirit."

EPILOGUE:
Ten Years Later

When *Good Morning, Holy Spirit* was published a decade ago, who could have imagined what would take place during the ten years since that date? Technological advances and mind-boggling inventions have brought radical changes to our world in so many areas including communications, medical science, business and industry, financial institutions, transportation, and more. These changes have brought convenience and comfort to millions in the natural and, more importantly, have provided the tools for the body of Christ to proclaim the gospel message to the ends of the earth as never before.

The last ten years have brought change and growth to Benny Hinn Ministries too. As the Lord continued to open more and more incredible doors of opportunity, the ministry headquarters moved from Orlando to the Dallas-Fort Worth Metroplex in 1999. Located at a major crossroads of the nation, the ministry headquarters is equipped to serve the partners and friends of the ministry efficiently while being strategically located to minister effectively from a central location.

Since that first publication of *Good Morning, Holy Spirit*, we've seen such wonderful new opportunities for ministry! The viewing audience of the daily television program *This Is Your Day!* has expanded to include broadcasts in more than 190 countries around the globe. The Health & Healing Channel was launched in late 2001 and offers contemporary and classic Christian programming on the topic of healing as well as a unique, cutting-edge approach from today's leading authorities on health, nutrition, and fitness. In addition to the domestic and international miracle crusades, this ministry has also begun holding special services for the youth of our nation. I am so grateful and humbled by what the Lord has done, and to Him belongs all the glory for what has been accomplished. The greatest preachers and prophets of days gone by have talked about and longed for these days when men, women, and children around the world would suddenly begin turning to God in unparalleled numbers, and it's been happening right before our eyes! What a tremendous opportunity for believers today.

Now, More Than Ever

I'm convinced, as I look back on the past ten years since *Good Morning, Holy Spirit* was first published, that we are moving into one of the church's finest hours in all of history. Christians simply must not miss this opportunity to tell the world and those who are looking for answers that Jesus is *The Answer!* In fact, if we falter, I believe God will hold us responsible.

With all this in mind, on the tenth anniversary of this book's publication, I am convinced that *now*, more than ever, two things are essential in the life of every believer: one, *the Holy Spirit's fresh, daily anointing* and two, *dying to self each day*. Let me share quick thoughts about each of these necessities.

Absolute Necessity Number One

Now, More Than Ever, We Need the Holy Spirit's Fresh Anointing

One of the most exciting, life-changing promises in the Bible is that the anointing of the Holy Spirit is available to each of us:

> Then Peter said to them, "Repent, and let every one of you be baptized in the name of Jesus Christ for the remission of sins; and *you shall receive the gift of the Holy Spirit. For the promise is to you and to your children*, and to all who are afar off, as many as the Lord our God will call." (Acts 2:38–39, emphasis added)

In this portion of Scripture, the apostle Peter clearly states that when we receive Christ, the power of the Holy Spirit is ours. To use today's wording, this precious Gift is part of the total "package." *The power of the Holy Spirit is included in the believer's inheritance.*

Since "the promise is to you and to your children," every believer worldwide must understand that the power of God not only belongs to us, but also to our children. And the promise of the Holy Spirit is for "all who are afar off, as many as the Lord our God will call." *Every believer is included!*

Here is the question: Have you ever considered why this promise of the Holy Spirit's infilling is so vital? I was pondering this recently and this realization suddenly hit me: *What would life be like without the Holy Spirit?* I quickly jotted down a list of sobering thoughts. Without a fresh, daily anointing of the Holy Spirit, here are seven impossibilities:

1. *It is impossible to know God without the Holy Spirit.* In Ephesians 5:18, we are told to "be filled with the Spirit." That's not a suggestion; it's a commandment! In fact, the Holy Spirit "bears witness with our spirit that we are children of God"

(Rom. 8:16). That measure of "knowing" requires a daily anointing of the Holy Spirit.

2. *It is impossible to understand the kingdom of God without the Holy Spirit.* Jesus said, "the kingdom of God is within you" (Luke 17:21). Paul the apostle taught that the kingdom of God is "righteousness and peace and joy in the Holy Spirit" (Rom. 14:17). God operates differently from man. As kingdom Christians, we are called to operate under a new set of thoughts, standards, and choices. Only the Holy Spirit's fresh anointing can help us understand this spiritual dimension that is hidden from the world.

3. *It is impossible to know the truth without the Holy Spirit.* Jesus talked about the Comforter who will *"teach you all things"* (John 14:26). Scripture also tells us that *"the Spirit is truth"* (1 John 5:6) and that the Holy Spirit *"will guide you into all truth"* (John 16:13). Falling into deception is possible without the Holy Spirit's constant teaching. The best and smartest of believers, even those who know the Bible from cover to cover, can be deceived if that person's daily relationship grows cold.

4. *It is impossible to stay free from sin without the Holy Spirit.* The Word of God declares that the Holy Spirit keeps us *"free from the law of sin and death"* (Rom. 8:2). Individuals who do not have a daily relationship with the Spirit of God open themselves up to weakness and falling into the sins of the past. Sin should not be allowed to have any power over believers, yet those who attempt to live the Christian life on their own are destined for failure. Perhaps you can think of someone who once loved Jesus, who sang all the praise songs, yet now they are out in the world doing the same

things they once begged God to take away from them. We must never shun the Holy Spirit's anointing and protection. We must seek the daily direction of the Holy Spirit, allowing the anointing of the Holy Spirit to touch us afresh each day so that we can stay free from the power of sin.

5. *It is impossible to pray with power without the Holy Spirit.* According to Romans 8:26, the Holy Spirit makes intercession for us. We pray in the Holy Spirit because we often don't know what to pray for, and He is faithful to bring our needs before God's throne. The Holy Spirit gives us insight during prayer that we would never understand without His leading. I never cease to be amazed at the believers who receive wonderful revelations during prayer for inventions, songs, business ideas, and breakthroughs. Too often we take this wonderful opportunity for granted. We need His presence both to survive and succeed.

6. *It is impossible to have a faith-filled life without the Holy Spirit.* Faith isn't something produced mentally. It's from the heart. Since it's from the heart, it's of the Spirit. He is the Source of faith. Without Him we tend to use our own wits, senses, and imperfect plans—then we miss His promises. According to 2 Corinthians 5:7, the witness of the Holy Spirit helps us *"walk by faith, not by sight."*

7. *It is impossible to live an unshakable, established Christian life without the Holy Spirit.* We must be "strengthened with might through His Spirit in the inner man" in order to be "rooted and grounded in love" (Eph. 3:16–17). Anything less than a daily anointing of the Holy Spirit leads to weakness and imbalance. It doesn't matter how busy you are, if you neglect time with God there will be consequences. You

must constantly be seeking the Lord and never rely on yesterday's experiences (see Lam. 3:22–25).

We don't have to live without the Holy Spirit or the impossibilities of being neglectful toward Him! With a fresh anointing of the Holy Spirit each day we can enjoy a possibility-filled life. In fact, if I have learned anything in life it is this: *We need the power of the Holy Spirit fresh and new every hour of every day. God does not give us "leftovers."* As God provided manna to feed and sustain the children of Israel in the wilderness, the Father offers us that precious anointing of the Holy Spirit that comes afresh every day, empowering us to live an overcoming Christian life.

As mentioned, I am more convinced now than I was ten years ago when this book was written that you cannot live *today* on what the Holy Spirit did for you *yesterday*. Thank God for the past, for each miraculous step that brought you to where you are today. However, what happened last week, last month, or last year will not sustain you today. Only claiming your inheritance of the Holy Spirit's daily anointing will help you overcome challenges and achieve great things for God.

Absolute Necessity Number Two
Now, More Than Ever, We Must Die to Self

As with the necessity of a daily infilling of the Holy Spirit and the precious touch of the anointing of the Holy Spirit, I'm more convinced today than ever that God is calling each and every believer to a life of total commitment and dedication. *Absolutely dying to self is the only way to total victory and success in service to the Lord Jesus Christ.*

Have you noticed that we rarely hear messages anymore about holiness and sanctification? Perhaps it's because there have been groups who have taught this subject in such a legalistic manner that it pushed people away from the church. That type of legalism isn't what I'm pointing to. Instead, I believe these biblical principles of holiness and surrender strike at the heart of everything we are today and will be in the future.

How important is the message of dying to self? The Bible, from cover to cover, points to this as the only way to a victorious life in Christ. As Paul wrote, *"I die daily"* (1 Cor. 15:31), and he spent much time teaching the church how to die to self. One of the most revealing passages is Romans 6:1–8:

> What shall we say then? Shall we continue in sin that grace may abound? Certainly not! How shall we who died to sin live any longer in it? Or do you not know that as many of us as were baptized into Christ Jesus were baptized into His death? Therefore we were buried with Him through baptism into death, that just as Christ was raised from the dead by the glory of the Father, even so we also should walk in newness of life. For if we have been united together in the likeness of His death, certainly we also shall be in the likeness of His resurrection, knowing this, that our old man was crucified with Him, that the body of sin might be done away with, that we should no longer be slaves of sin. For he who has died has been freed from sin. Now if we died with Christ, we believe that we shall also live with Him.

Over and over the Lord ties serving Him with dying to self. Self-sacrifice gives you victory over Satan, but self-saving or living for self gives Satan victory over you. That's why Jesus talked about dying to self so much. Saving yourself, keeping yourself, and protecting yourself ends up letting the devil have victory in your life. You simply cannot serve the Lord effectively and preserve self at the same time.

What does this mean? More importantly, how can you die to self as you seek to be empowered by the Holy Spirit—now, more than ever?

First and foremost, dying to self means yielding yourself to the Lord in everything. *Everything!* We often call this "repentance," which is translated as turning from sin and offering yourself on the altar for God to do whatever He wants. That's hard for humans to understand, and even more difficult to do as a willing participant. Yet it is required.

In the Gospel of John (12:24–25), Jesus spoke of His coming death on the cross and then taught how His followers would be required to give themselves completely:

> Most assuredly, I say to you, unless a grain of wheat falls into the ground and dies, it remains alone; but if it dies, it produces much grain. He who loves his life will lose it, and he who hates his life in this world will keep it for eternal life.

Why is it so important? The only people who have genuine authority over Satan are those who choose to go to the cross, to have self and sin nailed to the cross and to die to self. Dying to self is the *only* way to be victorious over sin, and the moment you yield yourself completely to the cross, you terrorize Satan!

When Jesus spoke these words to His followers, He was actually saying, "What happened to Me will happen to you." Real victory means following Him to the cross in total surrender. It means dying to your own ambitions and desires. Nothing less will do.

This kind of death takes place in the Spirit realm. Understandably, we don't literally get a hammer and allow our hands and feet to be nailed to a cross. This goes much deeper than physical pain. Spiritually, we must offer the "old man" to be sacrificed. That's what

Paul was speaking about in Romans 6:6 when he wrote, "knowing this, that our old man was crucified with Him, that the body of sin might be done away with, that we should no longer be slaves of sin."

Only by living a life of total dependence upon the Lord and by nailing the flesh to the cross can you live so sin cannot touch or control you.

How glorious it would be to live a life without sin. It is possible, for Jesus wouldn't have taught us to do something that we could never do. His life provided an example for us, and He gave us clear instructions on how we could live a life of holiness. And as you yield yourself completely to Him, your life will never be the same. Others will notice and lives around you will be touched for eternity as they see the changes in you.

Satan's ultimate goal for you is a cross-less life, and he would like nothing more than to get you to move in the opposite direction. Since his first encounter with man in the Garden of Eden, he has been attempting to deceive us into living for self in rebellion to God's laws.

Today he still promises kingdoms, power, pleasure, riches, and much more. "You don't have to die," he'll tell you, just as he taunted Jesus, as recorded in Matthew 4 during the Great Temptation. "I'll give you all these kingdoms," the devil urged, "and you don't have to go through Calvary. All you have to do is bow down to me. Then you can be the king without going through the sacrifice on the cross."

And if you do decide to crucify self, the battle really begins. The devil and his demons will do everything in their power to keep you from doing what you said you'd do. Only the power of the bloodstained cross threatens the forces of hell. Some Christians don't worry Satan, especially those who don't understand spiritual warfare, for they pose no threat to his kingdom. On the other hand, Satan knows the destruction you'll bring to his hellish kingdom the moment you say, "Lord, I yield myself completely to You."

You see, the moment you yield yourself completely to God, allowing your sins and your desires to be nailed to the cross, you terrorize the kingdom of darkness! The enemy knows you are slamming the door on him. The devil realizes that you are aligning yourself with the Father, Son, and Holy Spirit, as well as the angelic hosts.

Satan simply cannot win when you die to self. It strikes fear in his forces when a Christian reads and follows Psalm 118:27, "Bind the sacrifice with cords to the horns of the altar." It means dying daily to self. It means allowing the old man to be sacrificed on the altar. *Continually!* Most importantly, it's the one place where Satan cannot touch you!

Jesus' words to His disciples in Matthew 16 describe a most amazing exchange called *sanctification*, the word we use today meaning an ever-increasing participation in His death. It's a price few people are willing to pay.

If anyone desires to come after Me, let him deny himself, and take up his cross, and follow Me. For whoever desires to save his life will lose it, but whoever loses his life for My sake will find it. (Matthew 16:24–25)

Jesus pointedly said, "Lose your life and gain Mine." *What a miraculous exchange!* We hand in our "filthy rags" and unrighteousness, and in turn He gives us victory over sin, yet too often humans decide to avoid making the trade because we don't value what Jesus is offering. Oh, if we only knew the freedom and power that comes from total sacrifice and death of self.

The simple truth remains that without dying to self, there is no victory. The only people who have genuine authority over the devil are those who choose the way of the cross and dying to self daily.

Historic Times . . . Great Opportunities

Today, more than ever, God is touching hearts and leading the nations of the world back to Him. The biggest challenge before us is: Will you and I be spiritually prepared and equipped to respond to the needs of those around us who are searching for answers in a world of increasing uncertainty?

I pray that *Good Morning, Holy Spirit* will continue to help equip readers like you with a greater understanding of the One who has been given to endue you with power and authority to defeat the enemy. I believe the time has never been more appropriate for this teaching, for these are times of unparalleled opportunities to serve God as we share the gospel.

We live in historic days. We serve a God whose desire is to use us, His servants, to bring hope to the hopeless, to always "triumph in Christ" (2 Cor. 2:14) as we wage spiritual warfare.

May the Lord help you lose your life that you may gain His. As you lay down your own ambitions and die daily to self, may you move into a deeper relationship with the Holy Spirit every day to walk in the power and the anointing of the Holy Spirit—*now, more than ever!*

Study and Discussion Guide

Chapter 1: "Can I Really Know You?"

1. Has the Holy Spirit been a distant third person of the Trinity to you? What must you do to bring Him into your life?

2. What do people filled with the Holy Spirit look like? Are they somehow different? How would you recognize them?

3. Have you ever witnessed a healing, or other miracle, attributed to the Holy Spirit? What is your definition of a miracle?

4. What is the mission of the Holy Spirit among us?

5. If you want the Bible to come alive for you, what must you do?

Chapter 2: From Jaffa to the Ends of the Earth

1. Do you talk with the Lord in your prayers as if He was a good friend who stopped by? Practice spontaneous and open prayer right now.

2. Do you need to suffer for God to take you seriously? Why, or why not?

3. How do you interpret the author's dream about being a prisoner in chains and led down endless stairs?

4. In the same dream, what is the symbolism of the angel's appearance and the shackles falling from the author's hands and feet?

5. Does God use dreams and visions to send messages to "ordinary" men and women? Describe a dream that seemed to carry a message for you.

Chapter 3: "Tradition, Tradition"

1. What is God's plan of salvation for you?

2. Have you asked Jesus to be the Lord of your life? Have you publicly accepted Him as your personal Savior? If so, hallelujah! If not, what is holding you back?

3. Have you been ridiculed because of your Christian beliefs? How does your embarrassment or humiliation compare with the sacrifice of Christ on the cross, dying for you?

4. If your family members reject your Christian beliefs, what can you do? Name three things.

5. Is there a physical presence of the Holy Spirit that can be seen and felt in addition to a spiritual presence? What would be some signs of that presence?

6. Do you believe the Holy Spirit can heal any affliction? What is the scriptural proof of this?

Chapter 4: Person to Person

1. Are you ready to meet the Holy Spirit personally? How can you do this?

2. Just what does "being filled with the Holy Spirit" really mean?

3. List the ways in which you could think of the Holy Spirit as a personal friend.

4. Where is the Holy Spirit: in heaven or on earth? What is the scriptural basis for your answer?

5. Explain the Rapture. What is its significance for you?

6. Why is the Holy Spirit called the Holy Spirit?

7. The Holy Spirit is the One who_____, who _____ with me.

8. Is it proper to think of the Holy Spirit as the great teacher? Why?

9. What does the author say is the greatest sin against the Holy Spirit?

Chapter 5: Whose Voice Do You Hear?

1. How are you led by the Spirit?

2. How early in the Bible does the Holy Spirit first appear?

3. Define the breath of life that flowed through Adam's body.

4. What do we have in common with Adam, spiritually speaking?

5. Do you agree or disagree with the statement that "the Holy Spirit is God"? Explain your answer.

6. What is the scriptural proof that the Father, the Son, and the Holy Spirit are one?

7. Worldly people haven't a clue about things of the Spirit. Why is that?

8. Reread the seven kinds of communion with the Holy Spirit. What steps can you take to activate them in your life?

Chapter 6: Spirit, Soul, and Body

1. Complete this sentence: "I want to walk with the Holy Spirit, but can't because I . . ."

2. How does your church view the Holy Spirit? As an active or passive influence in our lives? Either way, what is the scriptural proof for that belief?

3. Of what form and substance is God?

4. Explain what the author means when he says the Holy Spirit has a mind of His own.

5. What is the temple of God as described by Paul in the New Testament?

6. Should the Holy Spirit be worshiped? Why, or why not?

7. What does it mean to vex the Spirit? How would we do that? How might we avoid doing it?

Chapter 7: Wind for Your Sails

1. Describe in your own words what a Spirit-filled life is.

2. What are the four main functions of the Holy Spirit when He is working in our lives?

3. What is the author's answer to people who ask him, "Am I filled with the Holy Spirit?"

4. At what point does the Holy Spirit become available to us personally?

5. Have you found it difficult, or impossible, to surrender yourself to the Lord? Try to pinpoint what is holding you back.

6. Write down the seven steps to meaningful prayer on a little piece of paper. Carry it with you, and refer to it when you pray. Try to include all seven steps until they become automatic.

7. If your prayers incorporate the seven steps, what is likely to come about in your prayer life?

Chapter 8: A Mighty Entrance

1. Do you have an answer in your heart to the personal question, What does the Lord have in store for me?

2. How can you find the answer to the previous question?

3. What is the Father's great desire for us?

4. Read the complete book of Acts. In your own words, write down God's plan for us.

5. What is the purpose of the signs that follow in the Holy Spirit's presence?

6. Is the Holy Spirit for everyone? Is He here today for you? How do you know? Read Acts 5:32; 10:44–46.

7. What is the foundation and authority for all the work the Holy Spirit was sent to do?

Chapter 9: Room for the Spirit

1. What is the most overlooked message of the church today?

2. Were the gifts of the Holy Spirit meant for us to use today? Explain the reasoning behind your answer.

3. What does the author mean when he says, "God is not weak—His people are"?

4. Explain the anointing. Name at least five people who have it.

5. What is the purpose of the anointing of the Spirit?

6. Describe how you can grow in the Spirit.

7. Was Jesus dependent on the Holy Spirit? In what ways, and why was it necessary?

8. What is scriptural proof that you shall have eternal life as Christ has eternal life?

Chapter 10: "Only a Breath Away"

1. What action must you take to receive comfort, peace, and direction from the Holy Spirit?

2. How does the Holy Spirit respond to people who willfully sin?

3. Define the separate roles of the Father, the Son, and the Holy Spirit.

4. How can we walk as one with the Spirit?

5. When you ask the Spirit of God to come into your heart, what are you doing?

6. It takes only five words to invite the Holy Spirit into your life. What are they?

Chapter 11: "Why Are You Weeping?"

1. Why can't blasphemy against the Holy Spirit be forgiven?

2. Read Matthew 12:30–32. How can you be assured you will never blaspheme the Holy Spirit?

3. How do you know the Holy Spirit is still with you?

4. Describe what it means to "walk after the Spirit." Read Romans 8:1.

5. For the next seven days, work on memorizing the seven works of the Spirit described by Paul in Romans 8. Write a short list of the good things that will occur when each work is manifest in your life.

Chapter 12: Heaven on Earth

1. Do you believe in healing by faith? Why, or why not? If not, state your reasons, not your feelings or emotions.

2. Whom does the Holy Spirit promote through His works? Is it you, God, Himself, or Jesus?

3. What is the source of the Holy Spirit's gifts?

4. How do you know when the *convicting power* of the Holy Spirit is working in your life?

5. The Bible says that the Holy Spirit has been given to you as a guarantee of _____.

6. What is the greatest purpose of the Holy Spirit?

7. Have you asked the Holy Spirit to come into your life? Have you asked Jesus Christ to come into your life? If not, you can do so right now by praying, "Jesus, I confess that I am a sinner. I believe that You are the Son of God and that You shed Your precious blood on the cross for me. Forgive me of my sin. Cleanse my heart from all unrighteousness. I thank You for saving me now. Amen."

ACKNOWLEDGMENTS

My special thanks to my dear wife, Suzanne, for her constant love and support.

My thanks to Neil Eskelin for his consultation and editorial work in the preparation of this manuscript.

I also wish to thank my loving mother for her prayers, which are a constant source of strength and encouragement to me. My appreciation also to Sheryl Palmquist for her editorial assistance, to Nancy Pritchard, my dedicated and loyal secretary, my brothers and sisters, and my dedicated staff for their assistance with this project.

About the Author

Benny Hinn is a noted teacher, healing evangelist, and best-selling author. His ministry reaches millions each week through his daily half-hour international television program, *This Is Your Day!* Tens of thousands gather at his crusades held throughout the United States and around the world to witness God's saving and healing power.

Hinn has written several bestsellers, including *Good Morning, Holy Spirit,* which has sold more than one million copies: *He Touched Me; The Anointing; Welcome, Holy Spirit;* and *The Biblical Road to Blessing.*

Hinn and his wife, Suzanne, reside in Southern California with their four children—three daughters, Jessica, Natasha, and Eleasha, and a son, Joshua.